THE I.T. LEADER'S FIRST DAYS

STARTING YOUR NEW JOB RIGHT

JOHN A. BREDESEN

Kennd

Kennd

Kennd Publishing
North St. Paul, MN
kennd-publishing.com

ISBN paperback: 978-1-7366500-4-2

Editor: Kristin Erlandsen
Cover Art & Illustrations: Dex Greenbright
Fonts: Adobe Garamond Pro, Proxima Nova

Publisher's Notes:
- Web sites used as links or references may change after publication.
- Search terms will return results that change over time. The publisher and author expect the reader to use good judgment to choose appropriate results to learn the concepts.
- Advice provided in this book may not be appropriate in your situation. Good judgment is required when applying any advice received from a book.

Library of Congress Control Number: 2022900783

First Edition
10 9 8 7 6 5 4 3 2 1

Dedication

This book is dedicated to those who love IT and wish to lead. This is a hard, but not necessarily lonely, road and the satisfaction of making a difference can be great.

CONTENTS

INTRODUCTION

It's time. Your hard work has paid off and someone has hired you to be a leader in an IT organization. You feel confident that you can handle the job. After all, it is something that you have been thinking about for a while.

Leading an IT group is difficult. Of course, you need to be up on the latest technologies and cyber threats. You need to know all the technology used in the organization and how to best use it.

You will lead a group of people. Maybe you have experience supervising others, maybe you don't. Whether your title is a lead, a supervisor, or a manager, your team needs to continually improve to better meet the needs of the organization.

You must know the organization well enough to make the right technology decisions, the right people decisions, the right priority decisions, and so forth. Living in the overlap between the organization and technology, IT plays a unique role, and you have a unique position.

Fortunately, I don't need to convince you that you need to learn. Holding this book in your hands is evidence of that. To give you the foundations and skills to be an effective IT Leader, I have laid out the book in the following chapters:

IT Leader Skills

You need to have some understanding of how you work. As a new leader, there are skills that will become more critical to your success. This chapter walks you through the ones I think are important. Exercises at the end of each section will help you develop these skills.

Your First Days

As a new leader, you only have a short time to orient yourself. You must quickly learn what is going on, what the challenges are, and what kind of team you have. This chapter lays out the work that you should do in the early days of a new IT leadership job to influence your future success.

Foundations

This chapter covers critical IT Leadership concepts: Change Management, Risk Management, and Focus & Finish. These concepts apply broadly to the situations you will face. Having a solid understanding will build a sound foundation for your leadership.

Business

If you don't understand the business of your organization, you can't be an effective leader. You need to understand the goals, how all the pieces work together, and where there are opportunities for improvement.

You need this understanding to lead the IT team to do your part to make the organization successful. Whether you work for government, the private sector, or a non-profit, this chapter will explain important concepts.

People

The people on the IT team are the most important component of the department. Technology comes and goes. The needs of the organization change over time. You must understand how to lead IT people effectively. Strengths, trust, and dealing with mistakes are important concepts.

Technology

Technology will change radically over the course of your career. Products and vendors will evolve constantly. This section provides you with some tools and thinking to manage the technology. I will provide you with a framework to think about technology and how to apply it to your organization.

I have spent over thirty years in the IT world. I have stepped into new IT organizations several times and learned how to manage existing teams and technical portfolios. I also have worked outside IT for almost ten years. I have seen the impact, both good and bad, that an IT department can have. I made my share of mistakes and learned from the many scars I earned.

Good Luck on your IT Leadership journey!

About This Book

→ I have collected all the resources in this book into a list at the back of the book for easy reference.

→ This book is part of *The I.T. Director Book Series.* Check out the series for other helpful books.

→ The chapters covering Foundations, Business, People, and Technology are related to the similarly named parts in *The I.T. Leaders' Handbook.* However, they have been distilled and substantially rewritten to benefit a new IT leader.

Chapter One

IT Leader Skills

Introduction

Going into your first leadership position, you won't have all the needed leadership skills. Clearly you have some or they wouldn't have hired you into the position. But you won't have these skills to the level that you will, say, ten years from now. These are skills you will work on to some extent most of your career.

If you are lucky, your organization will provide some basic leadership training. If not, there are leadership books available that can cover a lot of the basics.

There is also informal learning. Earlier in your career, you worked for various IT leaders. You picked up on their style, their skills, and their approach. Some of it will work for you, some of it won't. Your style and approach will be uniquely *you*. I view that as a good thing.

Some important tactical skills that I cover in this chapter will influence your style. You will use these skills daily as an IT leader .

When you fly on a commercial airplane, the flight attendants give a safety talk at the beginning of the flight. This talk contains a quote that frames up this chapter very well. During the presentation about the oxygen masks, they tell you to put your own mask on first before helping others. You can't help others if you are unconscious.

Similarly, as you are going through your workday, you will be less effective as a leader if you don't have the following skills:

1. Effectively manage your task list.
2. Effectively manage your work day.
3. Be able to learn fast.
4. Understand that everything is connected.
5. Be able to extract information from data.
6. Make effective and timely decisions.
7. Lead useful meetings.

Let's look at each one of these skills and how they help in your new IT leadership position.

Effectively manage your task list

As you enter leadership, you enter a world where you are primarily responsible for identifying and prioritizing your day-to-day task list. You won't be working on a project list. You won't be working from an agile sprint board. You won't be working on the list of help desk tickets. You will set most of your tasks, not someone else.

These tasks will be large and small. Some will depend on others and some will be only you. Some will be out in the organization and some will be with your team. Some will repeat and some will be unique.

You will need to maintain a sense of priority among things that are very short term (return a phone call) or very long term (set strategy for all IT systems).

Managing this wildly varying list is hard. Simple time management techniques can't handle this variety. It is also a very personal thing. Everyone has to find their own technique.

Unfortunately, I don't have a magic system to share as I have never found the "perfect" system. After a half-dozen time management classes, you would think I would have found the one true system to rule them all.

I did not. Because there isn't one.

But you need some way to track all the things you have to do.

Here is the most important part of a task management system: it needs to make sense to you. And only you. If you are one of those intensely organized people that have it all figured out? Great, you have a head start. If you are effective by managing your tasks using an app you wrote yourself years ago, great. If it is on blue paper with brown ink, great. Don't let anyone else tell you to do something different.

I am constantly seeking to improve, and I can say for sure that I am much better at it today than I was at the beginning of my career. But this will always be a struggle. Don't believe me? Ask around. See if you can find anyone that has used the exact same task management technique for over five years with no changes. I have met very few in all my years.

As I said before, task management is really hard.

So, what makes a good task management system? Since I can't (and wouldn't) prescribe any specific technique, I'll go a different route.

How do you know if you have a good task management technique? Simple (ha!). It should be able to do the following things:

- List the tasks that need to happen today, in priority order.
- List larger tasks and projects in a way that lets you define smaller pieces that need to be done today to keep things moving.
- Handle due dates. This can be difficult for many of your tasks, which won't have an external due date, only a due date you set for yourself. Remember that rarely does a day go completely to plan, so due dates will change.
- Deal with tasks that pop up and need to get taken care of each day. As a leader, plan for this to happen.
- Integrate with your email inbox either technically or by process. Everybody uses their email inbox as part of their task list. Only the Inbox Zero folks don't and there are very few people that do this for very long.
- Handle personal tasks. For example, pick up milk on the way home from work or call to make an appointment to get the air conditioner fixed.
- Handle regular occurring events. Examples include check-ins with other leaders, looking at financials, or reviewing vendors.
- Use the parking lot concept for ideas and other future tasks or projects that are not active. Some little corner of

the task management to capture items that may turn into tasks later.

There will also be "just do its" that have no place in your task list. An employee walks into your office and you can help them by sending a quick email, which you immediately do.

Once you have a task list you are working on and updating, you need to think about prioritization.

The three things I have found most useful for prioritizing are:

1. Determine if I am the only one that can complete this task
2. Eisenhower's priority matrix
3. Rocks, stones, pebbles, sand

Determine if I am the only one that can complete this task

There are tasks that no one else in the organization can do. Tasks like budgeting, performance management, and coordinating the overall work of the department. These types of tasks have one thing in common: you can't delegate them. You are the only one that can do them.

Everything else is a candidate for delegation. This doesn't mean that you must or can delegate, it just means that you should consider delegation.

Obviously, you need to be careful about dumping more tasks on your team. But perhaps you can structure some regular activities in a way to remove some tasks from your plate. For example, status reporting doesn't have to go through you if you are just passing information along to others. Look to your future leaders as candidates for this delegation.

Eisenhower's priority matrix

As President of the United States, Dwight D. Eisenhower had a lot of tasks to manage. Although he had a staff to help, he still needed a way to communicate priorities. To do so, he distinguished between the concepts of "urgent" and "important." Just because something is urgent does not make it important and vice versa. Let's look at his matrix.

	Urgent	Not Urgent
Important	Quadrant 1 React (fires, crisis)	Quadrant 2 Plan/Do
Not Important	Quadrant 3 Delegate/Outsource	Quadrant 4 Delay/Delete

Quadrant 1: Important/Urgent. Tasks that fall into this quadrant are daily tasks with deadlines and problems that come up. Pick up kids from school. Review the monthly financials that just came out. React to a system outage. Some days, you will spend more time here than you want. The tasks that show up in this quadrant are urgent, so you need to deal with them as fast as possible. You won't be able to take a long-term view when working in this quadrant.

Quadrant 2: Important/Not Urgent. You want to spend most of your time working on tasks from this quadrant. All your longer-term work falls here. The better you do on these tasks the fewer will make it to Quadrant 1.

Quadrant 3: These are urgent, but not important that you do them. For example, help desk tickets are urgent, but having you specifically work on them isn't important. Delegating these to more appropriate people will give you time to work on Quadrant 2 tasks.

Quadrant 4: Work to delay or delete these tasks. If they aren't important to your organization, your department, or you, why are they on your task list? Chances are good that they will sit at the bottom of your task list for a very long time.

Rocks, stones, pebbles, sand

Prioritization can feel overwhelming, especially if you are simply comparing priorities between tasks.

I suggest having a larger framework that you use for prioritizing. It won't solve everything, but it will help. What are the most important improvements for the organization? What are the priorities of the CEO? Does anyone on your team need special attention? These larger questions should inform your priority list.

If you spend all day firefighting, you won't be able to improve anything. If you spend all day improving things, some fires will not get the attention they need.

There is a concept that has been around for a while that I think can be useful.

Imagine a large glass jar. A big one. The kind that takes both hands to carry when empty. Next to the jar are some large rocks, a pile of stones, a pile of pebbles, and a large pile of sand. Imagine your job is to fit as much as possible into the jar.

So you try a couple of techniques. You put all the sand into the jar, then the pebbles, but you can only fit a few stones and no rocks in. You try a couple of other techniques.

Imagine your job is to fit as much as possible into the jar.

Then you try the rocks first. You are able to fit a couple of rocks in this time. There is empty space between the rocks, and you are able to fill that empty space with stones. You see there is empty space between the stones, and you add the pebbles. After that, you see there is still space between the pebbles, and you start pouring in the sand.

This technique—starting with the rocks first—is how you fit the most into the jar.

Consider the rocks to be the most important tasks you can be working on. These are your goals for the year or quarter. These are the tasks that will make the biggest impact on your team and organization.

As you probably have realized, the stones and pebbles are lower priority tasks that you still need to accomplish. And the sand? That sand is all the little stuff that pops up daily that needs to be done.

Set your task management process so that you make progress on the rocks first. The stones and pebbles after that. You will find that you still have time for the sand.

One version of this story has a twist I like. After the jar is full of rocks, stones, pebbles, and sand, you can still pour beer in. This illustrates that you can, and should, make time for yourself after all the work is done.

Your task management will be unique to you. And it won't ever be perfect. Pick something, work to improve it, and stay with it for a while. And don't worry if you keep trying different techniques to figure it out.

Exercises

1. Evaluate your current task management techniques. Does it match your strengths (e.g., paper or electronic)? Is it easy to keep updated? Fully implement a change that will make this process better.

2. Consider the different task list techniques you have used in the past (including just your memory). What worked well? What didn't work well? Talk to others to see what they use and grab the ideas that might work for your style.

3. Your inbox is part of your task management. How do you fit it into your larger task list? Do you get bogged down in your email instead of working on higher priority tasks?

4. Write down your goals for the next week. The next month. The next year. How are you making progress on each? How are these goals related to your task list? How do you make sure you are making progress on the important items?

5. What percentage of your task list can only be done by you? Can you delegate some tasks to your team?

Effectively manage your workday

In the IT world, and for IT Leaders specifically, we won't have time to get all our work done. There is always more work than we have time for. Managing our day is an important part of dealing with this.

I suggest two major steps to improve your productivity:

1. Control your interruptions.
2. Control your calendar.

Interruptions will happen all the time. Someone stops by your office with a question. You get a phone call you need to take. Someone stops you in the hall on your way to get coffee. Or worse, on your way to the bathroom.

Control these interruptions by starting small. Notifications from the computer and phone are not helpful. Turn most of them off. We don't need to know when each email comes in. Instead, set a few times a day to work through email.

If something is on fire and requires your immediate attention, email is not the right communication tool. People should call or come find you. By "immediate" I mean when minutes count. Email notifications present a false sense of urgency and are a distraction.

Smartphone notifications are even worse. Every time you install a new app, turn off all notifications except the critical ones. You control your devices, don't let them control you.

You control your devices, don't let them control you.

IT leaders get lots of calls from vendors. Don't answer them. Make sure caller ID works correctly on your phone and be ruthless in sending calls to voicemail. Respond quickly to those inside your organization, but outside callers can usually wait. Unless, of course, you are one of the rare IT leaders that work directly with Customers[1].

Next up, control your calendar. We have all kinds of meetings, from long-term leadership meetings to project meetings to department meetings. Make sure you are spending your time on the things at the top of your priority list. Sure, there are meetings you can't control, demands on your time that you can't do anything about.

Moving into a leadership position will provide you with more control. Team member one-on-one meetings, status updates, and department meetings will now be under your control. Use this to your advantage.

Be intentional about controlling the time that you have. I highly recommend blocking off time on your calendar. My style is to block off Monday mornings and Friday afternoons. A Monday morning block lets me get organized at the start of the week. And, for reasons I don't understand, I get weirdly productive on Friday afternoons.

---

1 Yes, I spell it with a capital C. See this article for more details: https://the-it-director.com/the-customer-is-our-only-customer.

Calendar programs are providing more sophisticated tools for setting aside this focus time. Learn how they work and use them.

Finally, not all hours of the workday are created equal. Portions of the day will be better for long, undisturbed thinking. Other parts, not so much. Learn what works for you.

I always struggle with the post-lunch slump if I am at my desk, so I try to schedule administrative tasks during that time. Since I get energy from meeting with others, I'll also schedule one-on-one meetings or walkabouts during this time. Conversely, I use the morning for longer uninterrupted time to work on larger tasks.

If you understand when you are strongest during the day, you can structure days accordingly. You will never have complete control over your schedule, but you have more control than you think.

Manage your days intentionally. You can't get wasted time back.

Exercises

1. Look at your last week. Did you feel good about what you accomplished at the end of the week? Why or why not?
2. Look at your last month. What percentage of time were you in meetings? Look at the meetings. How many could have been shorter?
3. Look at your larger tasks. Did you make progress last week? Why not? What will you do to make progress next week?

Be able to learn fast

An IT Leader position requires intentional and continuous learning. To survive in the IT world, you must continually learn. This is even more important for an IT Leader. There is always more to learn.

Everyone has different styles of learning. Reading, lectures, videos, and conversations are some options. Each of us processes visual, audio, and verbal inputs differently. We all learn by doing, but some of us like more frequent, smaller sessions and some of us like longer sessions. There is no wrong way to learn.

The time of day also matters. A deep dive learning session may need to be scheduled differently than watching a few short videos. The better you know your learning style, the more you can structure this into your calendar.

Larger topics are Quadrant 2 items and scheduling them ensures they get completed. Better yet, build these learning periods into your weekly and monthly calendars first, and fill them with topics later.

Learning topics will come from you. Rarely will someone give you a prioritized list of things you need to learn. You need to create this yourself.

Your new position will provide you with less time to learn new technology. You will rely more on your team to do the deep technical learning so you can focus on how the new technology fits into the larger portfolio.

Now that you have time to learn set aside, let's look a bit closer at learning.

Here is an analogy I use with new employees: There are sets of toys, including Legos(TM), K'Nex(TM), etc., that consist of small pieces you can assemble in an infinite number of ways. There are assembly instructions for one or two designs to get you started. Watching my children and grandchildren play, I saw them focus only on following the directions and building the "toy." It wasn't until they got older that they realized the individual pieces were the toy, and a car or house was merely one way to put them together.

In my basement, I have a bin of Lego pieces collected from all the Lego kits my kids had. There are thousands of pieces. The boxes and instructions are gone. All the kits are mixed together like the "punch" at a college party.

Imagine dumping them out in front of someone and saying, "These are all parts of a large thing. Start building."

This is like your new job. You have an enormous pile of blocks and pieces (products, services, departments, business processes, and so on) in front of you. No instructions. You might have a vague idea of how some of them fit together, but there is no picture on the outside of the box to build towards.

Actually, it is worse than that. No one collected all the pieces you need into one bin. You need to go on a scavenger hunt to collect them all.

Each of those pieces represents part of your learning. This person sends this report to that person. One piece. This system uses Single-SignOn for account control. Another piece. The HR system sends employee information to the payroll system. Yet another piece. Maybe the same assembly, maybe not.

Gradually, you build up larger "assemblies" in your head as you gather more information. Occasionally, you get an epiphany where two seemingly separate facts click into place to make a larger body of knowledge. Sometimes you realize there is a connection and go looking for it. Sometimes it is a surprise.

There is another facet of learning to point out: level of detail. Being intentional about what level you are thinking about and being able to move between the levels is important. Any one system, person, technology, or department is part of a larger system and also has a deeper level of detail within it.

The next thing to pay attention to is the level of detail. You have probably met people that are always diving into lower-level details. You have met people that are always going to the bigger picture, seeming to ignore the details. We need both views in an organization, but they are never the entire picture. Your job requires that you talk in both high- and low-level detail.

Your job requires that you be able to talk in both high- and low-level detail.

I find this to be one of the more interesting parts of my job. I can walk out of a strategic planning meeting and run into someone with a printer problem. I may then talk to the network expert about some DHCP or network load balancing problems we are having. Switching between the different levels of detail keeps it interesting and keeps me from focusing on only one side.

You, in your drive to be a better IT Leader, know that there is a time and place for both high-level thinking and low-level attention to details. Be intentional about what level of detail you are working on in any situation. A project planning effort should not get into the configuration settings. The financial state of the company has no bearing on a debug session. Those are easy ones.

The hard ones are when the level of detail floats around in a conversation. Sometimes this is good, usually it is less productive. Disagreements often stem from a difference in the detail level people are using.

In your new position, there are massive amounts that you need to learn. You will need to find all the pieces and assemble them into something that makes sense. You will need to learn the higher-level systems and processes and rely on your team to know the details.

Knowing how you learn is critical to your success.

Exercises

1. What was the last big thing you learned? How did you do most of the learning? What was the most helpful way to get the information?

2. What is the next big thing you need to learn? What is your plan? Have you set aside some time?

3. Get some Legos or K'Nex (or whatever). Make something that is not part of the printed instructions. Use as many pieces as possible. How did you fit the pieces together? How did you think about the design? Do you think top down or bottom up?

4. Pick a process, say Accounts Payable. Draw the higher-level diagram that shows where it fits into the larger organization. Draw the next level down diagram, showing more detail about the inputs, outputs, and actions of the process.

5. In your next meeting, pay attention to the level of detail being discussed. Who is thinking bigger picture? Who is thinking down in the weeds? What is appropriate for the meeting's goals?

6. Think back to your last conversation with a leader in your organization. What level of detail were they operating at? What level of detail were you are operating at?

Understand that everything is connected

In the prior section, we talked about how part of your learning is to realize that there are lots of parts and pieces that connect together. You will need to learn the business of the organization. You will need to learn about the people. You will need to learn about the technology. These are not three independent areas. Everything will connect.

Have you ever put together a picture puzzle? Maybe a 300-, 500-, or, if you are of a particular mindset, a 1000-piece puzzle? The colorful image on the box shows you what you are building towards.

In full disclosure, I have a love/hate relationship with picture puzzles. I love getting started, making good progress. Then I get impatient looking through the pile of pieces and I think to myself, "Ok, one more piece and I'll go do something else." Ten pieces later, I'll say the same thing. And I will keep going. Fortunately, learning at work is far more enjoyable for me. The pieces are more interesting and the connections more satisfying.

Most people use a certain process to put picture puzzles together.

First, we build the edge. Find all the edge pieces and then assemble the outside of the puzzle. This gives us a frame for the rest of the picture. All the other pieces will go into that frame. Then we build the interior using the specific image subjects of the picture. Using color, printed words, or some other visual cue, find all related pieces. Put them all near each other and then try to fit them together.

You may try fitting lots of pieces together to see if they fit. Try, fail, try, fail, try, succeed. This technique has you spending more time trying. Alternatively, you may stare at the pieces until you find two that look like they will match and then put them together. Try, succeed. Less time trying, more time thinking.

The reality will, of course, be a combination of both. Sometimes we will look and think, sometimes we will just try a bunch of pieces. We tailor our approach based on the situation.

When that last piece falls into place? Ah, sweet satisfaction.

Unfortunately, puzzles at work rarely have the "final piece" satisfaction, as they are never complete. The work puzzle is never-ending because the organization also changes over time. It's like trying to make a puzzle of a movie instead of a static picture.

It's like trying to make a puzzle of a movie instead of a static picture.

There are, however, more satisfying times along the way. Remember the satisfaction of connecting two long pieces of edging together? You haven't finished the puzzle, but you have made a major step. This happens a lot at work.

Given the complexity, there are many opportunities to connect larger parts of the puzzle together.

At work, you never have a picture of what the puzzle should look like when you finish. You can't reference an existing picture to see how a particular piece with particular colors may fit. As time goes by and you get more experience, you get a better sense of what each puzzle will look like.

The work puzzle is also never a clean rectangle. Every technology interfaces with other systems. In today's world, the outside edges of your technology profile get blurry with cloud services and integrations with Customers, suppliers, and governments. You will draw your own edges based on what you need to focus on or what needs improving.

Everything inside the edge you draw will connect to several others. Like a puzzle piece connects to four or more other pieces, people and technologies connect to each other in multiple ways. Every business process has inputs and outputs connected to other departments, processes, and people.

Earlier, I mentioned that the work puzzle changes over time. The history of the organization plays a major role in understanding the current state. Here are some examples:

- If your organization has grown quickly, there are likely systems that were designed for a smaller group of people and haven't scaled well. Manual processes that worked fine for a few dozen employees now struggle under hundreds.

- If your organization had a major restructuring in the past, there will be artifacts of the old structure in the systems. There will be reports that didn't get cleaned up and still present the data the old way. The network may still be segmented to match the former structure or former department locations. The old organization names will still be around in surprising places. For example, no one wants to change names of the file shares, so the old names stick around.

- If there were mergers or acquisitions, not all the systems will have integrated into a coherent whole. There will be different terminologies that didn't get merged completely, multiple naming conventions that still exist.

- If a major system was replaced by another, we will find remnants of the old system in the new system. Data structures and business processes will have been copied over rather than having been reimplemented from scratch.
- Old naming conventions started by individuals that are no longer in the IT department weren't carried on by those that followed.
- Architecture philosophies change over time. The computer industry has swung back and forth between centralized computing and some version of client/server so many times that both can look archaic.
- Email structures from the old email system were reimplemented in the new email system to make the transition easier for users.

People made decisions that were the best for the company at that time. Time goes by. Eradicating these historical artifacts won't always be worth the effort. However, ten years later, those artifacts will seem strange unless you know the history.

Figuring out how the business, people, and technology fit together is a never-ending puzzle. Fortunately, puzzles at work are interesting and the journey to understanding more of a joy.

Exercises

1. Put together a 300-piece puzzle. Note how you approach it. Think about something you are learning about at work. Are there similarities in how you go about it? Do you know where the edges are? Do you have a general idea of the picture that you will end up with?
2. Make a list of the major systems in your organization. What other systems do they interface with? Which groups of people in the organization work with the major areas of the big systems? How does time figure into the interface? Is the live data lookup or a scheduled batch data transfer?
3. Draw a map of your team. Circles for each person and lines between circles to represent time spent working

together. The heavier the line, the more they work to-gether. Add in the other parts of the organization they work with.

4. Look up *quote to cash*, *procure to pay*, or other major process definitions. Pick one and draw up the process map for your company.

5. How many systems use employee number or customer number as a key? How are the records kept in sync? How do all the systems get updated when employees come and go?

Be able to extract information from data

As an IT Leader, you will be awash in data. Data swirls all around. From your systems. From the business. From your team. That data is full of information that you need to manage the department.

Learn how to harness it.

First, you need to understand what you have. In your position, you have access to more structured and unstructured data than anyone in the company. That's a bold statement, but I believe it is true.

In your position, you have access to more structured and unstructured data than anyone in the company.

You (with help from your team, of course) have access to virtually all the data in all your systems. Finance and Human Resources may limit access to confidential data. But, generally, you have access to most of the data in the company.

Besides the data stored in application databases, you also have access to usage information that tells you how the company is using the systems. You have access to log files that may show transaction counts and related information. Think of these things as metadata that tells you how the systems are being used.

For example, you can pull usage information from one of your large systems. Usage is useful for determining exactly who is using the system. It can tell you who the heavy users are. It can tell you adoption rates on changes your team rolls out.

Your conversations with other leaders provide context to the data. The leaders provide goals for metrics. They are the ones pointing to areas that need to improve or express concern about trends. With this information, you have additional insights into what the data means.

Unstructured data, like priorities, external trends, and internal improvements, also provide critical context to the data. Others in the company have similar access to the data and the context, but they may not have the same level of data sophistication that you have.

Next, spreadsheets are your friend, get good at them. Know how to do lookups and pivot tables. Understand how to create useful graphs quickly. Practice. There are enough internet videos to get you going.

You will often just need to do some quick analysis. Being able to pull data in, do a pivot table, and draw some conclusions in just a few minutes is a skill that will benefit you time and time again.

Don't aim to be an expert at spreadsheets. Aim for getting fast at a few simple tasks that let you pull meaning from data.

Finally, understand the limits of the data. Being data-competent is critical. Being data-exclusive is a bad thing. You will always need to understand the context and limitations of the data you are looking at. Not everything can be explained by data.

Exercises

1. Grab some usage data from a system. This can be an application with usage logs or even something as limited as records with a creation date. Use pivot tables to determine your most frequent users, the busiest days of the week, and the general usage trend (increasing, decreasing, or flat).

2. Dump data from your help desk system. Find a category of tickets that is increasing. Find a category that has had no tickets in the last two months.

3. Explain the difference between correlation and causation. It will surprise you how often the two get mixed up in day-to-day activities.

4. Find an example of when the data changes meaning when placed in the proper context. Would someone have made a poor decision without that context?

5. What is happening with your organization's Customers? Can you find information that shows the markets the Customers sell into? Are those markets increasing or decreasing? Explain it to your team in a way that helps them understand the bigger picture of their job. This is a good example of unstructured data that you need to understand.

Make effective and timely decisions

As a leader, you will make more decisions. These decisions will be all along the continuum, from trivial to strategic. Some will be low risk; some will be high risk. You will need to decide which employees will do which tasks. You will need to decide which automation technology to implement. You will need to decide when to upgrade the ERP.

Some decisions will be easy. Some will be difficult. You won't have the quantity or quality of information you want. You won't know how the future should influence the decision. Sometimes you won't have any good options. Some decisions will be right. Some will be wrong. Some in the organization will always disagree with your decision.

With this breadth of scope, there is no set formula or decision framework you can simply plug everything into and have a decision pop out at the end. Search for "decision-making frameworks" and you will see many options, portions of which might be useful to your situation.

You will be well-served to think about how you make decisions. Which decisions are straightforward for you? Which ones do you struggle with? What type of decisions seem straightforward to you but not others?

One helpful way I have found for thinking about this is the maximizer/satisficer distinction.

Maximizers continue to look at solutions, even when there are multiple that specifically meet their requirements, until they are sure that they have made the best possible decision. Satisficers[2] (a blend of satisfy and suffice) choose options once they find one that meets their criteria. Whether the satisficer sets the criteria high or low, they will stop looking

---

2 https://www.merriam-webster.com/dictionary/satisfice

once the criteria are met. The maximizer, however, will keep looking until all options are exhausted.

Each of us is a maximizer for some types of decisions and a satisficer for other types. For example, I tend to be a satisficer for software as I believe that implementation has a bigger impact on success than the absolute best of the top two or three choices (presuming they all can do the job). I prefer to decide sooner and spend the time and money saved on a better implementation. But I tend toward a maximizer for decisions around system interface options.

I think this distinction has an influence on how you view inputs to the decision. Maximizers want to consider all aspects just in case they have missed something. Satisficers focus in on the core principles, values, priorities, and philosophies that apply and gather input on those areas.

For example, you may feel, as I do, that speed and flexibility are two important attributes of an IT department. Improving speed (of the organization) and flexibility is at the heart of many of the decisions I make and much more important than other aspects that may come into play. An option that has high scores for organizational speed and flexibility may look better to me than good functionality scores.

The opinions of others are also important inputs for your decisions. There will be those that have, in your opinion, thoughtful views on a topic and you choose to give their opinions more weight. There are those that are directly involved in the situation or process, and they bring a different perspective that you will need to understand.

The opinions of others are also important inputs for your decisions.

As you talk to others, you will see both sides of the decision. In fact, I would submit that, for larger decisions, if you can't present the case for both sides effectively, you don't understand the issue sufficiently.

So, how to make decisions? Rather than providing you with a framework for deciding, I will present major aspects of decision making and give you some approaches that will help.

Decision Scope
The scope of a decision includes the specifics, the stakeholders, and the timeframe.

If you can write a specific decision out in one clear sentence, then you understand the specifics. Getting consensus on that one clear sentence may be difficult but is necessary. The level-of-detail problem will come into play, as will each department's and individual's perspective. Don't assume everyone will agree.

If everyone who might care about the decision agrees with that one clear sentence, then you understand the stakeholders. This is tricky because the pool of actual stakeholders (people directly affected by the decision) is always smaller than the pool of people who think they are stakeholders. When the decision gets bigger, the number of wanna-be stakeholders grows exponentially. Distinguish between those you involve in deciding and those who need to be aware of the decision and the reasons for it.

A decision's timeframe covers two things: (1) When does the decision have to be made? (2) How long will the impact of the decision last? The first has to do with the speed of the decision and I will talk about that in a moment. The second is not always clear, but it is usually longer than you think it is.

If you focus on the long-term impact of every decision, analysis paralysis will freeze you. Instead, understand that the entirety of your decision making will affect the future. Your goals, philosophies, and strategies should be visible in the entirety of the decisions you make.

Sometimes decisions that you think you need to make are actually ones you can delegate. An example is time off requests. If you look into each request, making sure that projects keep moving, consider teaching your team to do that work before they submit the request.

Prioritization is usually a collection of decisions made multiple times a day that you can delegate. Teach your team how you prioritize and why you make the priority decisions you do. Eventually, your team can make those decisions on their own. The decisions will usually be as good and always will be faster than stopping in your office to ask.

Decision Reversibility

Is the decision reversible? Most decisions you will make are reversible. That means that you can fix any decisions that turn out wrong. Very few decisions are truly irreversible.

Sometimes it is new information that comes to light. Sometimes it is an estimate that turns out to be off. Sometimes it is changing priorities. It can be any number of things that make you realize that a decision needs to be revisited.

Reversible does not mean easy to change. But a decision that is hard to change is still a decision that can change.

Your ability to admit when a decision needs to change will have a massive, positive effect on your decision making. Read that sentence again.

A decision that needs to change does not mean that it was wrong. We decide based on our read of the situation and the (limited) facts we have. Facts change and our understanding is always changing. Getting hung up on "wrong decisions" gets in the way of doing the best for your organization. Getting paralyzed by the thought of a wrong decision hurts your organization.

Move past the concept of wrong decisions to the concept of course correction. You make a decision, the best you can make at that time, and some time down the road you realize it needs to change. You could look at it as a mistake, a bad decision, or a wrong decision. Your ego will inevitably start arguing with you and you will delay fixing the problem.

Course correcting means saying that as things sit today, a different decision needs to be made. Don't get hung up on the right or wrong of the original decisions. Make the course correcting decision and move on.

Of course, you have the opportunity to learn from every decision, especially ones you need to course correct. Understanding what changed is a good learning moment. Was it new information? Was it changing priorities? Was it a better understanding of consequences?

Legend has it that an IBM executive made a decision that cost the company $10M and didn't work out. Expecting to be fired, he went into his boss's office. But his boss talked instead about the $10M "education" the executive had received and focused on learning for the future.

You will make wrong decisions. You will make decisions that need course correction. You will make decisions that, down the road, make you say, "What was I thinking?" Don't let your ego get hung up on being wrong or dumb. Fix things, learn what you can, and move on.

This is important because you are modeling behavior for your team. If your team sees you don't get defensive when a decision needs changing, they will see a good example of how to course correct their decisions.

Simply being able to say, "Yeah, that decision needs to change," or even "I made the wrong call because I misjudged the schedule impact," does two things. It moves the organization forward faster, and it shows your team a better way than getting defensive.

Decision Risk

Reversibility of a decision is part of the risk of getting the decision wrong. Factors like money, time, implementation challenges, and so forth, raise the cost of a bad decision. The bigger the risk, the more effort you should put into getting it right.

This may seem obvious, but it is easy to get wrapped up in a decision and not realize that the risk of a bad decision is lower than you think. Or a quick decision you may be tempted to make has a larger risk that you missed.

One risk factor that is often downplayed or overlooked is Technical Debt (page 99). Be careful about this. Each piece of Technical Debt is a landmine waiting to go off in the future. If you care about the long term, which any leader should be, you will do your best to minimize this.

Decision Speed

When we decide can be as important as *what* we decide. Some decisions are not very important or are easily changed. In that case, you might take a "sometimes wrong, never indecisive" approach and make the call then and there.

Some decisions are best deferred. When you expect to have better information in the future, and most of the action from the decision is also in the future, consider delaying it. Or make a preliminary decision that can be erased and changed in the future.

Decision Implementation

For larger decisions, the implementation may be more important than the decision itself. A good decision implemented well may be better than the best decision implemented poorly. Unfortunately, organizations are often littered with the carcasses of badly implemented decisions.

Make sure the influencers in an organization understand the decisions and the

> *A good decision implemented well may be better than the best decision implemented poorly.*

reasons for them. The conversations they have with others will move the needle in the right direction.

Make sure all the processes that need to change to reflect a decision actually get changed, and the changes are effective. Processes are an engine for good in an organization, but they have an inertia that process owners must intentionally overcome for a decision to be fully implemented.

Exercises

1. Pick a decision you need to make. What is the timeframe for making the decision? What is the timeframe for the effects of the decision?
2. Are there any regular decisions you can be push to the team? Time off, task assignments, and so forth.
3. Pick several decisions that were hard for you to make. Write down scope (specifics, stakeholders, and timeframe). Are there any common themes? If this type of decision comes up again, is there a better way you can handle it?
4. Work with your team to identify a correct decision that was implemented badly. Discuss why it happened. What can you and the team do next time to implement better?

Lead useful meetings

Meetings are a force for good and evil in most organizations. We have all sat in meetings that were a waste of time. People didn't prepare. We made no decision. The attendees had mismatched expectations.

We have also sat in meetings that made a lot of progress and all concerned enthusiastically agreed on a decision. We enjoyed the daily standup that built a sense of team and comradery. It was great when cooperation overcame a roadblock.

As a leader, you will run more meetings. You will also be responsible for how well your team runs meetings. It makes sense to improve your skills in this area.

Here are the things I believe contribute to good meetings. Please note that there are few absolutes on this list. You still need to use your judgement for each situation.

Goal, a.k.a. "What is the point of this meeting?"

The goal needs to be very clear to everyone involved. The type of meeting (status, decision, brainstorming, investigation, or negotiation) sets the tone and expected outcome of the meeting.

Status meetings communicate the current state of something. The goal is for people to have better information that will allow them to do their job better.

Decision meetings should formally record a decision with documented evidence and reasoning for future reference.

The type of meeting (status, decision, brainstorming, investigation, or negotiation) sets the tone and expected outcome of the meeting.

Brainstorming meetings are useful for gathering options and opinions for a particular challenge.

Investigation meetings are useful for a small group to gather information from a larger group, such as problem solving or requirements gathering.

Negotiation meetings happen more than you might think. We know they happen with vendors. But in any organization larger than two people, meetings to negotiate through different opinions take place regularly. These can be especially important when large decisions with multiple stakeholders are on the table.

The goal of the meeting also sets the scope of the meeting. The meeting's scope sets the guardrails for conversion. If someone brings up something outside the scope, acknowledge the point, perhaps record it for future discussion, and then shut it down. It may feel rude, but keeping the meeting on track is the better choice.

Agenda

Every meeting needs an agenda. Every one. If you can't layout the steps the meeting should take, then you are not planning it well. If you are not intentional about the meeting plan, it will wander off out of your control.

Agendas don't need to be detailed, but do need to provide a general flow. For a 30-minute meeting, keep it to two or three agenda items. For a 60-minute meeting, you don't want more than five agenda items.

I recommend two items be part of every meeting, but they probably don't need to be listed on the agenda.

First, greet everyone at the beginning. Informal chitchat for the first minute or two to break the ice helps set the tone for the meeting. Don't underestimate your ability to set the mood for everyone with your opening words.

Second, close with a review of actions, decisions, or accomplishments that took place in the meeting. Thank everyone for their time and contributions. Show some appreciation. End on a positive note.

Respect for People's Time

You have now set the goal and agenda for the meeting. Who do you invite?

The first aspect of respecting people's time is to not invite them to meetings they don't need to be at. Of everything in this section, you will struggle with this one most of all.

The first aspect of respecting people's time is to not invite them to meetings they don't need to be at.

You should invite only those that are necessary and not one person more. This is a true, but unhelpful statement. Who is necessary? This is the challenging question.

To help you set the attendee list, ask yourself a few questions:

- Will this person contribute to the conversation?
- Does this person need information presented at the meeting AND there is no other way for them to get it?
- Does this person represent a group directly involved in the topic?

There are other questions, of course, but those should get you started. You will develop your own list of questions as you hold more meetings.

It won't be perfect. You will run into people that feel they should be at the meeting, but you, as the facilitator, disagree. You will run into people that won't want to attend a meeting that you feel needs their input. Make your call, review how it went, adjust your opinion as needed.

You also won't be the organizer of every meeting that involves you and your team. Those organizers will do it differently than you would. For example, I believe that an IT business analyst should attend early project concept meetings in order to get a deeper understanding of the problem. This puts them in a better situation when the project hits IT's front door. Not everyone agrees with this.

The second aspect of respecting people's time is to set the meeting length. In my experience, most meetings are scheduled for too long of a time. Add the fact that people think only in terms of 30- or 60-minute meetings, and you end up with wasted time. There is no law against having 15-minute, or 45-minute, or an hour and 15 minute meetings. Putting durations on your agenda items can help set the right length.

The last aspect is simple: start on time and end early. If you can get the reputation for doing this regularly, people will work harder to help you. Sometimes you may need to shuffle the agenda or delay a bit if a critical person is late, but try not to.

When you end a meeting early, you are giving the gift of time back to the attendees. Don't underestimate the value of this.

Have Fun

Seriously, have fun. Work can be a drag, the topic may be a painful one, and there might be a toxic person in attendance. Don't let those things put a damper on fun.

There isn't a specific recipe for having fun at meetings. Pay attention to what makes your audience smile and try to work it in. Set the tone yourself by being positive.

Everyone Contributes

Most meeting types need attendees to talk, whether it is to provide information or opinion. Not everyone will speak up equally. Some of us speak a little more freely than perhaps we should. Some tend to speak less in a group setting.

As a meeting organizer, you need to navigate this carefully. You can't let the loudmouths (like me) dominate the conversation. Sometimes you need to call on people to make sure you hear other voices.

But it may not work to call on people in the meeting. There may be good reasons for not speaking up that you don't know about. Some people also need time to process what they are hearing.

It won't take long for you to learn who the quiet ones are in your organization. Take the time to talk with them outside the meeting environment and hear their thoughts. If you talk to them beforehand, you can hear their concerns or input and you can bring it to the meeting. Or you can follow up afterwards to hear their thoughts.

The bottom line is not everyone acts the same in meetings and taking the time outside the meeting to make the overall results better is worth the time.

Exercises

1. Put a goal and agenda into your next meeting calendar invite. How did people react to it? Did it make the meeting better? Where you able to keep the meeting focused on the goal?

2. In your next decision meeting (or a meeting where a decision is made), send an email out afterward summarizing the decision. Include the inputs and reasonings that went into the decision. Put a good subject on it to make it easier to find it six months in the future when someone asks about it.

3. Schedule a 15-minute meeting and keep to it. How did it work? What did you learn?

CHAPTER TWO

YOUR FIRST DAYS

The first weeks and months of your new leadership position are crucial to setting the tone for the years that follow. People inside and outside the department get their first taste of what you are like as a leader. Chances are good that most, if not all, are rooting for you to succeed.

It takes time to come up to speed, to have a good grasp of the everything you need to know. My experience puts this at around 6-12 months. Organizations are complex, people are complicated, and IT is hard. This isn't something that happens overnight.

You have a grace period where they won't expect you to be up to speed on everything. During this time, you can ask all sorts of tough questions under the guise of being the new person.

Inevitably, people will expect you to have things under control. You will need to know everything your department does. You will need to know how the organization works. You will need to deal with all issues.

What if you could come up to speed faster than people expect, in weeks instead of months? What if you had a plan for those first days that helped you wrap your head around everything you needed to learn?

What if you could come up to speed faster than people expect?

This chapter lays out such a plan.

At the center of this plan are two words: *Listening* and *Learning*. You will be tempted to put plans in place and have answers for everything. Avoid that temptation at the beginning. Even if there are a few fires that need to be put out quickly, it will serve you well to take the time to listen and learn about the situation before deciding.

Listening means keeping your mouth shut and taking in as much information as you can; ask questions; read available documentation, presentations, and emails.

In-person or video meetings are valuable for learning tangible and non-tangible information. You will learn how they feel about other departments, including IT. You will understand what is important to each person. You will uncover their biases and blind spots. You will see how they think about their place in the larger organization.

Most of what you hear will, of course, be new to you. Take notes because you won't be able to remember everything. You will be drinking from a firehose of information and taking notes will help you retain more information.

Don't make the rookie mistake of pretending that you know all the answers. Coming in as a know-it-all sends a message to your new peers that you don't need their input. That's not a good way to build bridges to other leaders or your team.

This is especially true if they have promoted you to your new leadership position from within the organization. Your experience as an individual contributor and your leadership potential got you here. You already know a lot about the organization. However, the view from a leadership position differs from an individual contributor position. Leaders have to look further down the road. Leaders have to make decisions that impact the larger organization. Take the time to listen to and learn from others with a leadership eye and you will be better off.

Let's look at the major areas you need to cover:

- Learn about the Organization.
- Learn about the Finances.
- Learn about the IT Team.
- Learn about the Infrastructure.
- Learn about the Work.

Learn about the Organization

The IT department does not exist in a vacuum. Your department, and your job, exists to serve the larger organization. By understanding this larger context, you can make better decisions.

Start simple. Get access to the company organization chart with names, titles, and departments. Build a mental model of the organization so you understand where everyone and everything fits. Get access to a map of the physical building. Document your learning in whatever format makes sense for you. I like paper, so I can scribble notes as I learn more later on. Others prefer electronic note taking.

Schedule one-on-one meetings with the leadership team members and other key managers and individuals.

Schedule one-on-one meetings with the leadership team members and other key managers and individuals. These meetings will serve as anchor points for building your understanding.

Being the new kid on the block allows you some latitude that you may not have later on. Use it. "Hi, I'm the new IT leader and I would like to meet with you to learn about your department."

Practice good calendar etiquette from the beginning:

- Schedule the meeting in their office.
- Give the meeting a good title. Think about what the calendar invite looks like on their calendar.
- Include an agenda in the invitation.
- Start and end on time (unless they show a willingness to continue). An hour is a good start, as you can always ask to schedule another meeting if you both feel there is more to talk about.
- Ending a meeting early is a bonus for all concerned and starts building a reputation for not wasting people's time.

The bulk of the meeting should consist of you asking questions and then listening. If you are new to the organization, it may be worth spending a couple of minutes giving your background, but no more. Start with high-level topics but follow their lead for a bit if they go into details as it tells you what they think is important. As I said before, take notes because there is no way you will remember everything.

This conversation should not be about IT, it should be about learning the organization. Some of them won't be able to help themselves and will quickly drive to IT topics. Make a note of the topic and gently steer them back to the larger picture. Make it clear to them that it is critical that you understand their area of the organization. Put the IT topics in a parking lot for after your questions. Promise them a follow-up meeting to talk solely about IT if needed.

Study the org chart before the meeting. Memorize key names so you don't have to look up or ask during the meeting. This also shows that you have prepared for the meeting.

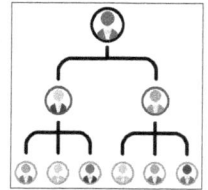

Ask follow-up questions. Ask for more information about a passing reference or something that isn't clear.

Repeat critical points back to them to verify understanding. People like to be heard and repeating their opinions or concerns back to them shows that you have been listening.

Let's look at some possible questions you can ask. You would, of course, list these in the calendar invite. Not for them to prepare, as they should know all this off the top of their head, but to signal what you are looking for:

- Tell me about your group. What functions does it provide and how does it fit into the larger organization?
- How would you describe the personality of your group?
- How is your group changing? What improvements are you trying to implement? What important improvements do you want to implement in the next few years?
- What other groups does your group work with? What works well and what needs improvement?
- Is there any important history about your group that would be useful for me to know?
- What is going well in the overall organization and what needs improvement?
- What external pressures is the overall organization facing?
- What business processes need the most improvement?

- What regulatory bodies or industry certifications are important to the organization?
- Is there anyone from your group that would be helpful for me to meet with to get a better understanding?

It is possible that you may already know some of the information, especially as you get further along with the meetings. You may have moved into a leadership position from elsewhere in the organization. Or you may have learned from some other conversations. In either case, stay quiet and let them lead. This allows them to talk about what is important to them and that is what you are really after. Even if they ask, tell them that yes, you are aware, but would prefer to hear their side of the story.

Now let's look at some of the IT-related questions you may ask. As I mentioned, these would be after the group and organization questions. Keep the focus of the conversation on the view from their seat, not yours:

- How does IT fit into the larger strategic picture?
- How does IT help your group meet its goals?
- Where does IT get in your way?
- How would you describe a good IT department?

After each interview, review your notes. The goal is to build a good working understanding of the larger organization. Over the next few months, refer to your notes with additions and clarifications as needed.

Your initial meetings should turn into regular touch-base meetings. This will keep you connected to the other leaders in the organization and keep your knowledge fresh as time goes by.

Learn about the Finances

$$$$

You now have budget responsibility for your department. Your organization will have its own terminology, but generically, you will have a department and a set of accounts (buckets) that finance will use to report your department's spending.

Ask the finance department for spending reports for the last few years. Start with whatever standard reports they issue. This will teach you about the reports you will see in the future and also won't take any extra time for Finance to produce.

Learn the spending trends for each account. Where is the spending increasing? Decreasing? Flat? I typically created a spreadsheet and entered the spending for the last few years so I could see the trends. It gave me a jump start on understanding the financials and is easy to maintain.

Ask for organization financial reports. Look at the bigger picture. Identify trends in organization revenue and spending.

There are two trends you should start tracking as early as possible:

1. IT spending as a percent of revenue over the last several years.
2. IT spending as a percent of total General & Administrative (G&A) spending over the last couple of years.

I prefer to track these numbers quarterly. Monthly has too much variation and annually isn't enough detail.

Knowing these trends will help you know the impact of IT spending on the larger organization. If you are lucky, there will be guidelines in which to operate. If not, you will need to set limits for the trends yourself.

If the organization is growing, you want to grow IT spending at a slower rate than the organization's growth. Aim for half the growth rate to allow more of the increased revenue to flow to the bottom line. If the organization is shrinking, you need to figure out how to shrink IT's budget to match the decline, if not more. As you might expect, staying in good communication with your supervisor and the finance department is critical.

A quick note about terminology. Terms commonly used are plan, budget, and forecast. Your organization will have its own vocabulary, of course, but here is how I think about it. The plan is set for the fiscal year and includes income and spending for the entire organization. The budget is your spending limits for the year. The forecast is what you think you will spend.

Big, complicated annual plans are becoming less important across the private sector, but may still be important for your organization. Life changes too fast these days for the annual plan to stay relevant for more than a few months. However, most organizations still do some version of an annual plan in order to set the budget.

Note that forecast and budget are different. You have limited control over budgets and more control over forecasts. Budgets are given to you (although you might have some input). Forecasts are created by you.

Do what is necessary to become good at forecasting. Understand all the components in your financial report and what goes into them. Maintain a list of all outside services, consultants, and cloud services and their future costs. If there is no framework from your organization, I suggest forecasting out fifteen months and updating the forecast each quarter.

The more the organization needs to change its business processes, the more work for IT, and therefore the bigger the IT budget will need to be.

Unfortunately, there is a lot of uncertainty when forecasting. What software changes will be needed? What ongoing expenses will there be for the new cloud system you may implement next year?

Even harder, the forecast is heavily influenced by what the rest of the organization expects IT to do.

Consider the organization as a moving vehicle. It is moving at a certain speed over a certain terrain. Improving business processes (page 71) causes the vehicle to go faster. The IT department gets involved with most major business process improvements. The more the organization needs to change its business processes, the more work for IT, and therefore the bigger the IT budget will need to be.

I think of the IT department as the throttle, the gas pedal, for the organization. Want to change faster? Press harder on the throttle. Do more business process improvement. Doing more improvements requires more IT spending (staff, consultants, software, and equipment). Need to cut costs? Let up on the throttle. Do fewer business process improvements which will require less IT spending.

Using the throttle metaphor, you can see it is important to understand what the organization wants to do in the future. You will need to adjust the IT budget and forecast accordingly.

Learn about the IT Team

As with learning the organization, one-on-one conversations are the best tool to learn the IT team. However, since these are the folks that you will lead on a day-to-day basis, you need a different focus.

Goal number one is to learn who they are personally. I'm not talking about grilling them about their personal life. That is none of your business. I'm talking about how they view work, their job, the department, and the organization. Learn what they know. Learn how they work. Learn what is important to them. Learn how they like to be recognized. Learn what annoys them. Learn what their job goals are. Learn who they connect with in the department.

You won't get all of this in one conversation. You will tailor these questions to each person. For example, you may ask for prior experience if they have been at the organization for a short time. HR may provide some of this information ahead of time, but it is good to hear it directly from each employee.

These conversations are more casual, so don't worry about listing questions in the calendar invite. Call it a getting-to-know-each-other meeting.

Getting to know each other is a two-way street. Plan on telling them a bit about yourself. A few minutes about your history and what is important to you at the beginning can help. Spend the bulk of the meeting asking them questions.

Besides getting to know them as individuals, getting their view of the department and organization is important. Here are some questions that may be useful:

- Tell me about your history at the organization.
- What is your experience with other companies?
- What does a typical day look like?
- What does this department do well?
- How would you describe the team's personality?
- Tell me one or two things that you think that I, as a new leader, should know about the department and the organization.
- How does the rest of the organization view IT?

If you have these meetings in the first week, as I strongly suggest you do, the team may be hesitant around you. You are, after all, a stranger to them and you haven't built up trust yet. Don't push it. Listen. Echo back what you hear on points that seem the most important to them. Trust will come over time as they learn who you are and how you work.

I want to say a few words about the situation where you are promoted from being a member of the team to being the leader of the team. This is a difficult position to be in.

You are now supervising your peers. Some of them may have also wanted the position you now hold. Some of them may think they know you well but hadn't previously noticed your leadership qualities.

Even if everyone on the team feels you will make an excellent leader, they (and you) are used to having a certain relationship. That relationship must change. I'm not talking about being friendly, respectful, or helpful. I'm talking about the fact that your words should (must!) carry more weight than they did when you were a peer. Be clear about suggestions and expectations.

You will want them to keep you in the loop as their manager more than they needed to when you were a peer. Make this part of the conversation so everyone is clear.

Be intentional about how that relationship will change.

One technique I have used over the years is the "working with John" stuff. Each of us will be unique in our leadership style and being clear on expectations is helpful.

Let's say that I am having a conversation with a team member, Ron[3], and I want to talk about how we work together. I need to know how to best manage Ron, and Ron needs to know my management style. The conversation might include the following statements:

- Ron, here is a "working with John" thing. You don't ask me for time off, you tell me. You are an adult and I trust you to manage your own time off. Just make sure that I and the rest of the team know. And make sure all your projects will be fine during your absence.

---

3 See "Names from the Examples" on page 119 to learn about the names used.

- What do you need from me so you feel more comfortable prioritizing your work?
- When I need an estimate from you, do you prefer an email or stopping by your office?
- What have your past managers done that really annoyed you?

The goal here is for you to have a better understanding of how your team works. And for your team to have a better understanding of how you work. By discussing these topics ahead of time, we can avoid unnecessary confusion.

I recommend monthly or quarterly one-on-one meetings to talk about bigger picture with your team. These are not the regular check-ins you should also have to talk about current projects and problems. The focus of these one-on-one meetings is to look at the bigger picture.

In *First, Break All the Rules* (Marcus Buckingham and Curt Coffman, Simon & Schuster), the authors lay out twelve questions you should regularly ask your employees. While they all can be useful, I focus on two of them.

Do you know what I expect of you?

Expectations are a key part of a successful working relationship with your team. Each employee must know what their supervisor expects of them. Regularly asking this question will reduce misunderstandings.

Asking this question will force you to be clear about expectations. There is a difference between an expectation and a desire. Try to have only a few expectations and work to keep them clear.

For example, I have an expectation that the team communicates schedules with the rest of the organization. "I'll have that to you next Tuesday." "We will have the change request complete by the end of the month." But my expectation does not include any how or what. It can be email, phone call, or a scribbled note. If asked, I will provide guidance, but I generally leave that up to them.

Do you have what you need to succeed?

This question covers a lot of ground. Office space, software, information, hardware, support, training, relationships, and much more. Anything the employee thinks they need in order to do their job.

You likely will need to throw out ideas as most will not understand the scope of the question.

Learning about the team is an ongoing effort because people change. Talk to each member of your team frequently. They are the ones that are doing the work.

Learn about the Infrastructure

In American football, the athletes who are in the offensive line positions rarely get the glory. There are rarely positive highlight reels on the game recaps. Often, they only get attention when something goes wrong.

However, as many coaches will tell you, as goes the offensive line, so goes the offense. The positions on the offensive line require understanding complex blocking schemes and instinctually reacting to defensive schemes. They require extreme speed and flexibility—all while weighing over 300 pounds.

Infrastructure is IT's offensive line (except, of course, for the 300 pounds part, that is not a requirement). As goes the infrastructure, so goes the organization. Infrastructure is highly technical. The people and the technology need speed and flexibility. It requires a good plan in place and the ability to react to changing needs and threats.

As goes the infrastructure, so goes the organization.

Unfortunately, like the offensive line, there are rarely any positive highlight reels. You don't see articles on how an organization has a great infrastructure. Others in the organization rarely appreciate a solid infrastructure unless they realize that they never have any problems.

Now your job includes overseeing the infrastructure.

This includes hardware: networks, servers, storage in the data center, and the fleet of computers and laptops distributed throughout the facility and in remote locations. It includes software: operating systems, backups, DNS, DHCP, Active Directory, or some other security/identity tool, cyber-security, and dozens of small utilities. There are cloud systems that your organization uses. There is often an off-site disaster recovery site. Hopefully some of this documentation exists already.

What follows is a quick overview of each of these areas and some guidelines to get you started.

Physical Architecture

Start with a high-level view, preferably one or more diagrams that describe the physical components of your infrastructure, including cloud systems. Such a diagram and supporting documentation should show at least the following:

- Network connections for both internal and external network connections, including vendor information
- Disaster recovery/business resumption facilities and equipment
- Critical server names such as DNS, DHCP, Active Directory, and cyber-security tools
- Physical and/or virtual servers
- Major storage systems

Physical Infrastructure Guidelines

1. Assume that each device will fail at some point. Use risk assessment to determine if you need to eliminate your single points of failure.

2. Your naming scheme for DNS and DHCP should be consistently used everywhere. The number of devices on the network gets very large and these naming schemes are the only way the infrastructure team can keep their sanity.

3. Beware the lone individual that keeps much of the information in their head. This is a risk to the organization no matter how good the employee. Consider using a Help Desk person who wants to grow into system administration to keep the documentation updated.

I.T. LEADER'S FIRST DAYS

4. Keep updated support information available in a single, well-known place for all major systems. When something breaks, you don't want to scramble to figure out who to call. This includes phones numbers, email addresses, and basics of the support plan like hours, response time, and covered components.

5. Your lists of servers and workstations (computers, laptops, tablets, etc.) must be automatically generated and maintained. Trying to keep them updated manually simply won't work when the numbers get large. There are tools at all price points to do this effectively.

Security Architecture

Security is foundational for today's IT department. The moat around the castle (a.k.a. a good firewall) is necessary, but no longer sufficient. You must assume the bad actors are already inside your network and include security and account controls throughout all your systems.

Learn all the components of the security architecture. Understand what they protect and what they don't.

Consider creating a security team that meets regularly and always has one security improvement active. This should be someone from your infrastructure team, from your business analyst team, and someone from the Help Desk. The goal with this team is not to implement massive security changes (although they are a great core for those efforts), rather the goal is just to keep improving security.

Security Architecture Guidelines

1. Employees and external account holders (typically vendors) are a large security risk. Put a training program in place, with periodic testing, to keep everyone's skills up.

2. Even if you are not required to implement them, there are security standards that are worth following. Consider ISO27001, NIST 800-171, or comparable standards. They provide an excellent overview of best practices. These standards won't tell you what to im-

plement. Instead, they cover security areas that you should address.

3. Turn on encryption for your network and for all storage at rest.

4. User account maintenance is a critical task. Onboarding and offboarding should use automation to create/disable user accounts. Control vendor access with special account naming conventions and auto-expiration. Use quarterly reviews of active accounts to make sure that nothing sneaks through the cracks.

5. Service accounts are accounts created to be used by programs and utilities. For example, a utility that reads from a database every night and creates a report. These accounts should have the bare minimum permission sets so they can't do anything other than their specific task. It is better to create many service accounts with small permissions than taking the lazy way out and creating one service account with elevated permissions. The extra security risk is not worth it. Where possible, prevent interactive login to the account.

6. Pay close attention to your super-accounts. This includes administrator accounts, ERP administrator accounts, etc. Best practice is to minimize who has those accounts and change passwords frequently or switch to multi-factor authentication for them. Never use them for service accounts.

7. Application accounts are just as important as your network accounts. An internal bad actor can do immense damage to one of your central systems. Use timeouts, password expirations, and multi-factor authentication for your larger systems. Use the "minimum permissions needed" concept everywhere.

Use the "minimum permissions needed" concept everywhere.

I.T. LEADER'S FIRST DAYS

Application Architecture

The servers, storage, and networks in place serve only to run applications. This includes everything from the basics like email and calendar to your central systems like ERP or client services that are fundamental to your organization.

Application Architecture Guidelines

1. Keeping an updated list of applications in use at your organization is massively useful for many things. I have used it for maintenance tracking, operating system compatibility projects, knowing who uses each application, and tracking versions. Start your list, make sure everyone maintains it, and you will find many uses for it.

2. All major systems should have a good test system. The more improvements your organization will make, the more the test environment will be useful. Put some effort into streamlining the update process so you can frequently update the test environment from the production environment, including data.

3. Test environments for large systems are great places for training and learning. If you are cloning production into your test environment, user accounts get cloned also and new employees will have a playground to work in before changing data in the production system.

Disaster Recovery/Business Resumption, including Backups

Problems and mistakes happen. These can be significant or trivial events. We lose the data center because of a hurricane, fire, or power outage. We lose a file because of sloppy clicking.

These may seem like different events, but the systems we put in place need to handle this kind of range.

As an overly-simplistic definition, I look at backups as making a second copy of your data because we should never trust having just one copy of anything electronic.

Disaster Recovery (DR) and Business Resumption are two different terms that, at a low level, mean two different things. But at a high level, both are just your organization's plan for when something terrible happens.

IT can, and should, have a plan for dealing with the loss of a data center. This plan is necessary, but insufficient. The organization must have a plan for all the rest. People, processes, and other normal operations need to be included in the Business Resumption plan.

Disaster Recovery, Business Resumption, Backups Guidelines

1. Setup exception reporting from your backup system. It should provide a list of true errors to the Help Desk. Any errors should get reviewed and fixed by the Help Desk or escalated. A large portion of backup system problems show up early in the logs, but sometimes no one is looking and the warnings are missed. Yes, I learned this one the hard way.

2. Track the normal "Hey, can you restore this file that I accidentally deleted?" activity as tests to the backup system.

3. Record failures in your systems as tests to your DR system. This is especially important when you have failovers in place that need to be tested. If the internet connection goes out, did the network failover to the backup connection? If a hardware server goes down, did your virtualization system handle it as you hoped?

4. See if you can work DR testing into your regular schedule. For example, once a quarter, switch over the DR site, run for a bit, and then switch back. This takes extra work to set up but gives you confidence it will work when truly needed.

Vendors

In today's world, vendors play an important role in IT. In the past, we only bought hardware and software from the few vendors we used. Today, every vendor has professional services (a.k.a. consultants) that are useful under some circumstances. Cloud companies are, at their core, service companies with the quality of their service indistinguishable from the quality of their products.

Review the vendors that are used by your department. Review the contracts. Review how much you are spending with each vendor. Separate the vendors into two lists: (1) Transactional and (2) Strategic.

Transactional vendors need little attention. Resellers like Amazon, CDW, or others fall into this category. Easily switched if you find another company that offers similar products at better prices.

Strategic vendors take more attention. These will be your ERP vendor or a consulting house that you regularly use. Put in the time to understand what you are spending and what you are getting.

I will cover this topic more in the Technology chapter.

Vendors Guidelines

1. Go through your list of vendors with your team and divide them up into transactional and strategic. Don't worry about the gray area, move a vendor to one or the other based on how much attention you or your team think they will require.

2. For each strategic vendor, understand what they are doing for your organization. How critical are they to your operations? How important are they to future improvements?

3. Set up meetings with each strategic vendor. Have them give you their standard pitch for new customers so you get a feel for what they emphasize.

4. As I will discuss in the Vendor section (page 94), look for places where there is a mismatch between what their core strengths is and what they are doing for you. Wander around their website and meet with the sales rep to understand their strengths. Are you using one of their strengths or a minor side product or service?

Learn about the Work

The last big topic to learn about is the IT team's work: active and up-coming projects. Team interviews will tell you about active projects, including scope, schedule, costs, and risks. If you are lucky, there will be an accurate list somewhere. If not, create one and keep it maintained. I provide the list of types of IT work in a later chapter.

Future work is a little harder to uncover. There might be a few projects that are already queued up with a project manager assigned and definitions of success defined. There is likely more work that is partially defined and not prioritized.

It is the unscheduled, unplanned projects that are the toughest to identify. These ideas can exist anywhere in the company. Add a question to your organization interviews to uncover these.

Projects can be a challenge to your prioritization list. For example, an ERP upgrade will stop most of the other requests your team works on. The team simply won't have time or the upgrade will require a technical freeze window. It will frustrate the employees that need those requests.

There is a concept called "opportunity cost" that is useful to use when thinking about what your staff is, and can be, working on. Opportunity cost refers to the cost of what *isn't* being worked on.

Opportunity cost refers to the cost of what isn't being worked on.

Let's say that you have a team member named Michael. He is finishing up a change request and there are two high-priority changes that fit his skill set at the top of the queue. Let's call them Change1 and Change2 to keep things straight. Using the Focus & Finish concept (covered in "Focus & Finish" on page 59), you will only assign him to work on one of those changes: Change1.

Change2 is obviously important or else it wouldn't be high priority. The benefits of Change2 to the organization may be time, efficiency, quality, or monetary.

Opportunity cost refers to the delay of these benefits. Sometimes you can quantify it, for example, hours/day in efficiency gains. Sometimes you can't.

By putting Michael on Change1, the opportunity costs for that decision are the Change2 benefits that are now delayed. If Change2 will save

100 hours of work per week, a four week delay will have an opportunity cost of 400 hours.

Now imagine that you have another employee, Stephanie, that can also do Change1, but isn't the best fit for Change2. Assigning Stephanie to Change1 and Michael to Change2 allows both to get worked on.

Of course, there will always be Change3, Change4, and so forth waiting in the queue, so you will never eliminate opportunity costs, but you can reduce them.

Projects often have a larger opportunity cost, as they involve multiple people for longer periods of time. There are more tasks that aren't getting done because the project is active. Similarly, assigning four people to spend five months on a new application will keep them from working on other changes during that time. Note that there is always an opportunity cost for any decision, no matter how "right" the decision is.

Your role, besides making team assignments, is to communicate all of this to the rest of the organization. In fact, opportunity cost must be part of the larger conversation when laying out the large projects your team will work on for the next year or two.

Stepping into a new IT leadership role, you will learn about projects that everyone wants, and hopefully will be involved in prioritization. Lay them out on the calendar and look at your staff. The better you can map it out and communicate it to the rest of the organization, the more you can manage expectations, including opportunity costs.

The rocks, stones, pebbles, sand story (page 8) applies here. Setting the rocks for the department before other priorities ensures that the most important work gets completed.

For tasks that are smaller than projects, think about the process of prioritizing and completing them. I call these non-projects Change Requests. The change request process needs to cover the following:

1. How change requests come in
2. How change requests are prioritized
3. How change requests are executed
4. How change requests are closed

Focus on getting the process right and work with your team to implement the process. Sure, you will get involved from time to time in specific change requests, but the more your team can operate independently, the better.

To make the prioritization process smooth, consider these options also:

- Spend time making sure that your team understands the larger organizational priorities and the internal IT priorities. This is an ongoing activity. Doing so will help them deal with all the new requests that come in.
- The backlog of change requests should be visible to everyone, as should active change requests. This will help the organization understand everything that IT is being asked to work on. There are lots of benefits to that.
- Pay attention to how your team keeps others in the organization aware of progress, schedule changes, technical issues, etc. This is often fertile ground for mentoring opportunities.
- Drive improvements to the Change Request process by presenting the problem or area of improvement to the team and letting them come up with ideas and solutions. This will increase their ownership of the process.

Summary

You won't be able to do everything in this chapter at once. You will need to put a plan together for how you will get all this done in your first days.

In Michael Watkins' book, *The First 90 Days*, there is a great chapter on accelerating your learning. The chapter's stories and explanation of learning have been useful to me when I changed jobs. The importance Watkins places on learning is clear. "Accelerate Your Learning" is chapter 2 of the book (chapter 1 is about getting yourself mentally ready). Learning is your best investment in your future.

One last note about your early days in a new leadership job. I call it the "Three Month Tsunami" phenomenon. On day one, you don't know what you don't know. It is like standing in an abandoned shopping mall that has no power. You can only see what your flashlight shines on.

Your concern is primarily about what you don't know. You are concerned about the unknown but you don't know how big it is.

After about three months, you have learned much about the mall, er, your new job. You know how big it is. You are aware of most of the spaces out there, but you haven't explored them all yet. You know a lot compared to your first day. But now you also know all the things that you *haven't* learned yet. You know everything that you have yet to learn, everything that you need to take care of, and all the problems that are in play now or will be shortly. You transition from being concerned about a vague unknown to being concerned about a specific and large list you still need to learn about. This can feel overwhelming.

Hang in there. You will get through it. The next section will give you some foundations that you will find useful in managing the tsunami.

Chapter Three

FOUNDATIONS

Architects create long-lasting buildings built on sound foundations. The best athletes excel in the basic skills. Musicians have mastered the basics for their genre. A sound foundation is necessary for long-lasting excellence.

As a new IT leader, there are important concepts and skills for you to understand. They are not about any particular technology or type of business. Instead, they will apply to almost everything you will do in the future.

I will provide an introduction to four concepts:

1. Continuous Improvement
2. The Square Root of Change (Change Management)
3. Focus & Finish
4. Risk Management

Some of this is new thinking, some of it is an introduction to well-known concepts.

By having a clear understanding of these four foundational concepts, you will have a solid foundation for your IT leadership.

Continuous Improvement

The concept of Continuous Improvement (CI) is central to each of us as a person, both at work and in our personal lives.

We start out as children, learning about the world around us. We continuously learn and start walking, talking, and soon we are using complex handheld devices to shoot imaginary zombies or tweet tiny messages to people on the other side of the world.

We would never have gotten where are without continually improving at this thing called life.

There are two primary facets of CI that I want to talk about. Neither of them is the formal definition[4] with acronyms and fancy methodologies. This is something much easier to understand:

1. Personal CI—What are you improving about yourself?
2. Organizational CI—What are you improving about the organization?

Let's talk a look at each of these.

Personal CI

Let's look at Personal CI. To be specific, let's look at CI for your work skills. As you read through this book (and do other learning), you will probably have several areas you want to improve.

Pick one or two and work on them. You don't need to attain perfection in something. Just get better in a way that improves how well you do your job. Then move on to another topic.

Be intentional.

Frequently, your personal CI means changing your habits. Building up new habits means breaking old habits. This is hard and you can only do it intentionally. That is why they are so hard to change. It must be an intentional effort.

There are a variety of techniques to help create new habits, but this one has been most successful for me:

---

4 https://en.wikipedia.org/wiki/Continual_improvement_process

- Phase 1: Identify the situation after the event where you wish to create a new habit. Identify what you should have done. Gradually shorten the time between the event and identifying that it happened. Remember that these are habits, so you aren't necessarily thinking about them in the moment. Make a point of watching for the event.
- Phase 2: You are remembering, in the moment, that you want to create a new habit. You may start the old habit, remember, and then pivot to the new habit. Repeat this. If you miss one and use the old habit, go back and do it right (the new habit). Keep repeating.
- Phase 3: The new habit is in place and you are no longer thinking about it.

Task management is another area that you may wish to improve, especially early in your career. At least once a year I try to improve this skill. Some years I make big changes, some years I make minor changes. Years accumulate and I am much better at task management than when I first started.

Continually taking small steps to improve yourself will result in large gains over the years.

As the word *continuous* implies, you will work on personal CI your entire career. Continually taking small steps to improve yourself will result in large gains over the years.

Organizational CI
Organizational CI is a harder thing and requires more planning and effort to implement.

The culture of the team affects everything, including CI, and therefore the improvements you can implement.

Influential business management expert, Peter Drucker, reportedly said that "Culture eats strategy for breakfast." There are a variety of ways to interpret this as it relates to CI. Here is mine: the culture of the team affects everything, including CI, and therefore the improvements you can implement. Let's unpack that a bit.

As a leader, you identify several improvements you want to make in the department. One of the great, and common, disappointments of new leaders is when they communicate the improvement and expect the improvement to be perfectly implemented the next day. The reality is that teams don't work that way.

Let me speak to the peanut gallery for a moment. Yes, you can use hard-ass tactics, yelling and screaming, to get people to improve immediately. Fear works amazingly well. But fear only works for a short time. After that, people will leave or stop thinking for themselves. Neither of those two responses will result in the improvements you want.

Ok, back to our department and the improvements we want to make. Since you are smarter than the manager using the fear tactic, you explain the "why" of the improvement to the team. And you immediately see the first facet of culture. How does your team view CI? Are they enthusiastic or skeptical?

Here is a way to think about this. Consider a bus. The bus represents the improvement, the change, you want to implement. Everyone on your team is initially on the bus, living the status quo. After you explain the improvement, a few of them will jump off the bus, run to the back, and start pushing to make the change happen. These are the people that support the improvement and actively want to make it go faster. There will also be a group that jumps off, runs to the front of the bus, and starts pushing backwards against the change. This is the group that does not want the improvement and actively works against it.

Most people will stay on the bus, undecided. They aren't working against the improvement, but they aren't working for it either. They are passive.

The more people you have in the back of the bus pushing, the faster the improvement happens. Depending on how big the improvement is, it may take a while to get any speed.

In a larger group, pay attention to the thought leaders in your group. It is possible that some people pushing in either direction are there because they are following a trusted peer. If you can explain the reason for the improvement to a thought leader that is pushing against you, you may flip them and the people that follow them.

The culture of the team will cause them to be predisposed for or against improvements. Fortunately, culture is not a fixed thing that you have to just accept. As a leader, you can influence culture. If there isn't a culture of continuous improvement, start building one. Use your team and individual meetings to promote the idea of CI instead of a specific change. Be patient, this takes time.

I talked earlier about how fear doesn't work. What works much better are clear expectations, teaching, and mentoring. Explain to the team that you expect them to get better and why. Bring them into the discussion about what needs improving. You likely have some smart people that already know some places the team can improve.

The more ownership the team has of an improvement, the faster and better it will get adopted. Set a goal for the improvement and explain why, then let the team figure out how to meet the goal.

Sometimes you have to get out of their way. I had a group of business analysts that didn't like the system we used to manage our change requests. I put forth that we needed to get faster and better at implementing change requests. They proposed replacing the system as their *how*. I was skeptical. It wasn't about the system being used; it was about how they used the system, and they weren't talking about that.

However, they were all in an agreement and had a plan to implement the improvement quickly. I stepped back from my opinion and gave them the go ahead. Part of the culture I was trying to build was *faster & better* and they were confident the new system would help.

It did. The team became faster and better. They met my improvement goals. They became faster and better at implementing change requests.

My skepticism was wrong. By stepping back to the values (CI and *faster & better*), I kept the focus on what was important as an outcome. The team determined the *how* and implemented the new system in short order, improving the change request process. The metrics we implemented around faster and better showed the improvement.

Not all improvements will be as large as a new system, but like with personal CI, small improvements over a long time will result in big improvements.

You will find it hard to prioritize improvements in the IT department. Like the shoemaker who can't make shoes for their own children because they are too busy making shoes for everyone else, the IT department can often be too busy helping others to improve our own processes.

Change Management: The Square Root of Change

IT is a complicated mix of stability and change. Your systems need to be stable and they need to work as expected all the time. And, at some point, everything will need to be improved, upgraded, or replaced.

This balancing act is hard to manage. It gets difficult when we change anything that the others in your organization interact with. Changing anything with a user interface will get a wide variety of reactions. Remember the change bus we covered earlier? Changing something familiar will get a lot of users out in front pushing back against the change.

Having a good mental model of how users deal with change can help you implement the change more smoothly.

The Square Root of Change is a good starting place for understanding what you will put your users through. I came up with this concept back in the 1990s after I had struggled through some implementations that went badly.

Early in my career, I was leading a project to switch 2000 users to a new email system. The new system had more functionality, a better user interface, and a brand-new calendaring system. I was young (and foolish!) and thought the change was good! And exciting! I figured the users would love it, right? Wrong! A few enthusiastic folks did, but many weren't happy with the change, and they swamped the Help Desk with complaints and perceived problems. The transition took months with significant disruption.

What did I do wrong? Two things: I didn't understand that change is hard, and I didn't listen to the users.

What did I do wrong? Two things: I didn't understand that change is hard, and I didn't listen to the users. Two thousand users got switched over, but the switchover was more painful than it needed to be.

I knew I needed to figure out a better way. Looking back on other projects I had worked on, there was a pattern. The benefits of the change never showed up immediately after the change.

And the Square Root of Change was born.

To start, consider that all changes are made to improve something. We need to stay focused on that improvement.

Look at the image below. Imagine some sort of measure of productivity as the left axis. The bottom axis is time. Before implementing the change, we are at one level of productivity and, after implementing the change, we will get to a higher level.

It doesn't have to be productivity. It can be response-time, it can be error-free client interactions. It can be scrap on the production floor.

The critical, and unavoidable, part of the illustration is that there will always be a dip in the measure when the change occurs. This dip will always happen, and you cannot eliminate it.

Square Root of Change

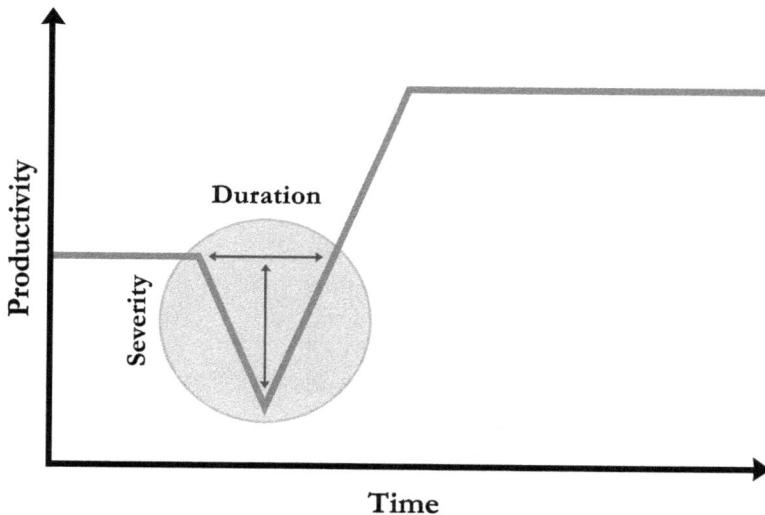

You can, however, reduce the dip. There are two aspects to pay attention to: the depth of the dip and the length. The depth is the drop in productivity. Users will think of it as how bad things will get. The length of the dip is the time it takes to get back to the starting level of productivity.

When you are planning the project, find the users that are concerned. Find the ones that are worried about it, or think it is a bad idea. The ones that say, "Well, what about...?" Find the ones that are in front of the change bus, pushing backwards.

Listen carefully to their concerns. They will have valid points that you need to address. The true test is this: can you correctly echo back their concerns to them (and the project team)? If you can't, you don't understand it well enough and need to keep learning. If you can, you likely will have already thought of how you can address the concern.

Addressing these concerns will reduce the dip by reducing the drop or the duration. You don't have to get them to be enthusiastic about the change. That will never happen for some. Aim for them to see that you have changed the project in a way that addresses their concerns. Don't ask, "Does this take care of your concern?" Instead ask, "Does this reduce the difficulty of the change?"

Said another way, the people that are complaining the most about the change can be your biggest ally in making the change better.

By making the dip visual and potentially quantifiable, the Square Root of Change gives you a way to think about changes that allows you to make them faster and with less disruption.

Focus & Finish

Focus & Finish should be your mantra for managing the number of active change requests and projects. Simply put, have a very small number of active tasks and make sure that each one gets completed properly.

Have a very small number of active tasks and make sure that each one gets completed properly.

Let's look at "Focus" first.

The standard IT situation is to have more change requests and projects in the queue than the team will have time to complete. Some will have deadlines. Some will be nice to have. Some will come from inside the company. Some will come from Customers. Big, small, simple, complex, and all flavors in between.

The first step is to prioritize them. I'll cover that later in the book, so for now, presume that you have everything nicely prioritized.

So, you and your team get started on the list. Yes, I know it isn't a clean start as some are already underway and the team is already fully busy. But I'm going to describe the situation slightly artificially. Real life will be more complicated, which will reinforce my point.

Your team won't work on one change request or project per person. Each person will work on several at a time, and here is where the problem lies.

Focus & Finish

What is the right number of active change requests or projects?

There isn't a perfect number for everyone, but I can guarantee that the number that gets the best through-put is less than you and your staff think.

You see, multitasking is a myth. You must "Focus" on a few active tasks.

I am not talking about music-in-the-background-while-writing-code multitasking. I'm not talking about listening to an audiobook while on your commute.

I am talking about switching between the tasks that, individually, should take all of your focus. Most change requests and projects that IT works on fall into this category.

Every time we switch between these tasks, we lose time as our brain reloads the details, remembers what needs to be done, and gets back up to speed.

Think of a pit stop in a car race. The car has to come in, make a complete stop, wait for the work to be done, head back out pit row, and then accelerate back up to race speed.

Think of a woodworker that builds custom tables and chairs. Imagine if they started cutting wood for a table, then stopped halfway through and partially stained a chair, and then changed to designing a complete set on the computer, but went back to cutting wood before finishing.

The obvious price being paid in all these cases is the switching time. No matter how big or small the task, switching from one to another takes time. It is simply less efficient than completing one task before starting the next one.

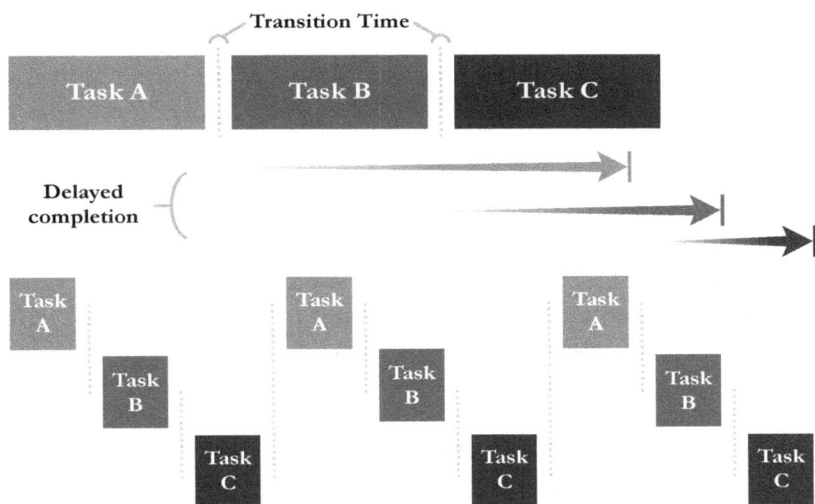

If you have lots of tasks open, you might go a week or two before getting back to one of them. What are the chances that you will remember everything exactly as you left it? Zero. You will have to recreate your prior state, your prior decisions, your prior subtask list.

Inevitably, someone will stop you in the hall and put something on your to-do list. Perhaps they mention something, and you nicely say, "I'll look into that and get back to you." If you don't write it down, there is a good chance that you will forget it before you get back to your desk.

The English language has lots of phrases describing the situation where there are too many open tasks:

- Too many irons in the fire
- Biting off more than you can chew
- Too many balls in the air
- Spreading yourself too thin

Other languages and cultures have their own with the same implication: it is not productive to work on too many things at once.

You and your team need to focus on a small number of open tasks to get the most done.

"Finish" is the second part of "Focus & Finish" and refers to fully completing a change request or project.

The team is working to get new functionality into production as soon as possible. Since they are working on the most important requests from the business, and the organization doesn't get the benefits until it is in production, the "go live" date is the schedule driver.

However, rarely is "go live" the last task you need to complete. Source code needs to be organized and closed down in the repository. Training needs to be given. Documentation for new employees needs to be updated. Lessons learned need to be documented to improve the next project. There is always something after go-live.

These post go-live tasks are not glamorous and won't be high on anyone's fun list. The next project on the list looks all shiny and new and exciting. The temptation is great to cut corners and skip the last few tasks.

Each task we skip is a little trap that we have left for the future. If it truly doesn't matter, then why was it on the task list? We may or may not stumble on it someday, but why do that to ourselves? Just finish the work.

This is where a lot of Technical Debt (page 99) comes from. As we will see later, Technical Debt is just unnecessary future work that we are leaving for ourselves.

Focus—keep a very small number of tasks active.

Finish—finish each task completely before starting something new.

It applies to you and your daily task list.

It applies to your team and the organization's projects they are working on.

Focus & Finish.

Risk Management

Risks are bad things that may happen in the future. A server may go down. A kid may fall while riding a bike. A hard drive may fail. You may get a flat tire while driving. An interface may error when receiving unexpected data.

These events may or may not happen. When they do happen, it may be a small thing or a major problem.

We manage risk in our everyday life, we just don't do it formally. Most of us have a gut reaction and then rationalize afterwards. We rarely do a written risk assessment and then intentionally mitigate, or reduce, the risks. Sometimes we over- or under-emphasize a risk because we don't take the time to put it into context.

Folks designing medical devices, airplanes, and rockets follow a more formal process. This formal process ensures that all significant risks are mitigated.

During part of my time working outside of IT, I worked in the medical device industry. I learned about the formal process of risk management and the tools it involves. When you look at the number of medical devices in the world that work safely, even when they break, the formal process clearly works.

While you may not need the formality of the medical device risk-management process, you need a deeper understanding of risk to be an IT leader. So, let's look at some basics and see how you can apply it to your job.

There are four aspects that characterize a risk:

1. Likelihood—what is the chance that the risk will happen?
2. Severity—if the risk happens, how severe is the outcome?
3. Detectability—if the risk happens, what are the chances that it will be detected before the bad things happen?
4. Risk Factor—in the formal risk management process, this is calculated using likelihood, severity, and detectability to arrive at an overall score which is used to determine if we need to mitigate (reduce) this risk.

While you won't use risk factor in the IT world too often, understanding the concept helps.

Typically, likelihood, severity, and detectability are rated as a number (for example: 1,3,5) and multiplied together to get the risk factor. Minor risks end up with a low risk factor, major risks get a high risk factor. In formal risk management, any risk-factor number higher than a preset threshold triggers actions to mitigate likelihood, severity, or detection.

Here is your takeaway for IT.

To reduce the impact of a future risk, you can

- Reduce the likelihood of the risk event happening,

- Reduce the severity if the risk does occur,
- Reduce the impact by detecting the risk event before it causes the bad outcomes.

So, what does all this mean for you?

First, detectability is an important tool. If you can detect that the disk is getting too full before it fills completely, you can fix it before the system goes down. If you can detect a network problem as soon as it happens, you can start repairs faster than if you wait for your users to tell you about it.

If your department doesn't have a good monitoring tool, get one. There are open source options and commercial options. Start with open-source until you and your team have a good sense of what, and how, you want to monitor.

Expand your idea of what can be monitored. Disk space, networks, servers, and firewalls are the first step. Monitoring security, applications, and processes are next steps which can really reduce the firefighting your team has to do.

When you roll out new technology, implement monitoring from the start. You may not know everything that needs to be monitored at the beginning. Simply run through the list of risks with likelihood and severity to identify good monitoring possibilities.

Monitoring security, applications, and processes are next steps which can really reduce the firefighting your team has to do.

Reducing severity is also important. We are familiar with this in our personal lives, as we all know about seat belts and bike helmets. The downstream implications of potential IT problems are not always as clear or as easy to mitigate. Start with the downstream risks, and then go up the causality chain. You will see areas that need more attention.

We can rewrite a failing data import job that is preventing other tasks from running. We can add better data integrity checks to eliminate planning software errors.

And, of course, likelihood is something we all understand fairly well. Or at least think we do. Ask ten people about the likelihood of something happening and you will get different answers. This is true in real life and true in IT.

But the main point still stands. If a risk event will cause significant trouble, reducing the likelihood is important. For example, a common problem in IT is not getting access to the appropriate people for requirements definition or testing. Depending on the change you are implementing, this may or may not be a major risk. If it is, having conversations with the managers can ensure the right people are available when needed.

Make sure you understand how to do risk assessment and look for ways to mitigate the bad risks. You won't need the formality of numbers, risk factors, and spreadsheets. You will need to run through the risks in your head and know which ones need mitigating.

Chapter Four

BUSINESS

Your new job is to lead the IT team. You and your team are the experts about applying technology to help the organization, much like the Human Resources department is for people, and the Finance department is for money.

Chances are you came from inside an IT organization and have experience with a variety of technologies. Ideally, you will have some sense of how the technology benefits the organization, which requires that you have some sense of what the organization needs.

This becomes much more important when you are a leader. As I will explain in the first section of this chapter, it becomes your most important job.

The next section covers business processes, the fundamental way to think about how an organization does its day-to-day work. Some processes are simple, with a few people and tasks, some are more complex. Some have a lot of automation, and some are completely manual with little documentation.

If the organization is going to improve, these business processes must improve. Knowing how to define and manage a well-functioning business process will put you and your team in a good place to help the company improve.

Of course, changing business processes leads to work for IT and I cover managing this work in the last section.

Your Most Important Job

In a 2021 interview, Elon Musk said something very applicable to your new leadership position[5]. He was asked a question about the development philosophy behind Starship, Space-X's rocket, then under development. Musk has previously described the Starship development philosophy as: try lots of ideas, fail fast, learn quickly, and continuously improve.

Describing the process, Musk said, "A guided missile is going in the wrong direction at any given time. But it course corrects. You don't want to be a super-precise cannonball when you don't even know where the target is."

I think this sums up IT leadership pretty well. There are very few fixed targets you can count on being in exactly the same place in a few years. We must constantly course correct to stay pointed in the right direction because the right direction is always changing.

You lead a team with lots of connections to the rest of the organization. You lead a team that supports the technology and process needs of the entire organization. You will make priority decisions and resource allocation decisions that affect the entire organization. How can you do these things if you don't understand the entire organization?

You can't.

And that fact leads me to this statement: Your most important job is to understand the organization well enough to lead the IT department to deliver the services necessary to meet the organization's needs. Yes, your most important job is to look *outside* the IT department at the larger organization.

Yes, your most important job is to look outside the IT department at the larger organization.

You can only be an excellent IT leader if you have a strong understanding of the organization. This understanding will help you direct IT for the next weeks, months, and years. Knowing the changes the organization is facing tells you what new technological solutions may be needed or what applications won't be able to keep up

5 See "References & Recommendations" on page 110 for details.

with those changes. Knowing the organization's strategy tells you what projects and other changes will be important. You can put people and technology in place to support those decisions.

Like a cruise missile uses radar, GPS, airspeed indicators, and so forth to see the terrain in front of it, your knowledge of the organization will tell you what is in front of you and your team.

Here are three things to learn about the organization:

First, know all the major departments in the company and have regular meetings with the leaders. Can you draw a high-level organization chart from memory and say what each part of the organization does? Can you do the next level down? The answer needs to be yes.

As I discussed in "Learn about the Organization" on page 33, meeting with other company leaders is important. Meeting once is useful for getting off to a strong start. Meeting regularly is necessary to maintain the relationship and to stay in touch with what is happening in all areas.

Second, know the overall finances. The top-level P&L (profit & loss) statement can tell you a lot, especially if you have access to history. This applies to business, government, non-profits, all organizations. Is there more of an issue with money coming in or money going out? Is one department's expenses higher than they should be?

If you have a small amount of knowledge about the P&L, you can tell a lot about what financial pressures the various departments are under. This gives you insight into some future projects that may help. For example, if a department is growing and needs to add headcount, maybe some automation would be helpful. If revenue needs to grow faster, are there some sales systems or processes that IT should help with?

Learning to read a P&L, by the way, is much easier than some of the technical information you have learned in your career. Find a friendly finance person and have them walk you through it.

Third, your team knows a lot about the organization. Use it to build your understanding. What they know will be smaller bits gathered from the front lines of the organization, and will differ greatly from the larger view you get from other leaders and from the P&L.

In an earlier chapter, I used the Legos(TM) and K'Nex(TM) toys as an analogy for your learning. Lots of little pieces of information build up a larger picture of the organization. Your team can provide you with additional pieces.

For example, your help desk is in a great position to learn about what employees do. They absorb a lot as they are solving problems, probably more than they realize. You will need to ask specific questions to get to that information.

But if you teach them to be curious and to ask questions of the people they are helping, they can learn more. Examples of such questions could be

- What do you use this application for?
- Why is this printer critical?
- What and when do you print?
- I'm curious, what does your department do? What do you do?

Your business analysts and project managers are also a source of information. They spend most of their days improving business processes—they can't help but learn about how the organization works.

The requests in IT's queue are sources of information. Talk to the requestors and understand why a request is important. Dig into the motivations behind it. Look at all the requests from a department to see patterns and trends.

Let's look at some other ways to build this deep knowledge of the business:

1. Get in the regular habit of walking around the facility and talking with people. Take the long route to and from meetings. If you work in a manufacturing company, make a point to walk the production floor regularly and make connections with those you meet.
2. People like explaining what they do and what challenges they face in their job. Use this. If you ask questions of enough people, and listen carefully to their answers, you can understand the organization better. Much like a pointillist painter, you can create a large picture from the individual dots. Can you see commonalities? Is one group unknowingly making another group's job hard-

er? Is there functionality that multiple groups can use to solve a set of problems?

3. Your peers in finance and human resources see the organization from a different angle than you do. Talk to them regularly.

4. Is there usage data for applications? How is it changing? For example, people might be using a particular data set more in the last six months. Usage information tells you about how the organization is using the solutions your team has put in place. It may contain a signal of changes in the organization that you might not otherwise see.

5. Some organizations have daily cadence meetings for front-line workers. IT attendance at these meetings, even if not every day, helps IT members stay current on issues. For example, some manufacturing companies have "tier" meetings. Ten-to-fifteen-minute meetings for everyone, followed by hierarchical meetings with supervisors and managers. These meetings allow issues to escalate in minutes instead of days. These meetings can teach you about common problems and situations. They can also give you earlier notice of some upcoming requests.

6. People need information to do their jobs. If it isn't available in the way they want, they will create it themselves. Find out who creates manual reports. Why are they sending it out? Who do they send it to? What do the recipients use it for? This can tell you where your reporting systems are not meeting the needs of the organization. It also helps you understand the decisions and actions driven by the report.

7. Learn about and embrace any Shadow IT. They are doing it for a reason and that can tell you more about that department. Remember, one of the big reasons Shadow IT exists is the organization believes IT is too slow, and rarely is that opinion wrong. My book, *The I.T. Leaders' Handbook*, has a section on how to partner with Shadow IT instead of viewing it as an evil.

I.T. LEADER'S FIRST DAYS

There are other techniques that can be on this list. Anything that gives you more information about what is happening in the company and the outside environment will help.

The more you know about your organization, the better you can do our job. You need to take all the information, stories, and complaints and turn them into strategies and tactics for driving the IT department. You can help the business only if you have a strong understanding of the organization.

Business Processes

All organizations use business processes to get work done. Most business processes in larger organizations will rely on computers and software. IT's role is to make sure the business process, as implemented in technology, change as the organization changes.

This requires that IT understands the business processes well enough to do our job correctly. Some examples of business processes are:

- Sending a quote to the customer,
- Designing a custom product,
- Responding to a complaint,
- Receiving payment and recording it correctly,
- Handling an IT Help Desk ticket,
- Onboarding a new employee.

Notice that the last two are from the IT department. We will come back to those in a moment.

A business process has one or more inputs, some activity by one or more people, and one or more outputs. In larger organizations, we store all the inputs and outputs in computer systems.

Therefore, IT is critical in today's organizations. Not only do we need to understand these processes, but we must also

Not only do we need to understand these processes, but we must also understand the technology that enables them, so that we can improve them as the organization requires.

JOHN A. BREDESEN   PAGE 71

understand the technology that enables them, so that we can improve them as the organization requires.

There are two types of processes: (1) normal processes and (2) exception processes. Normal processes do the work of the organization. Exception processes handle the situations where something goes wrong. Looking back at the example list above, the Help Desk ticket is an exception process (something has gone wrong) and onboarding is a normal process.

Why do we call out exception processes? Because the goals differ from the goals of normal processes. The goals of an exception process are to

1. Change a situation back to a normal or acceptable state.
2. Record the root cause of the problem, if possible.
3. Provide data that allows the prevention of future problems.

Looking at the Help Desk ticket problem, you can see how the first goal is true. People usually contact the Help Desk when something goes wrong or breaks. Help Desk personnel work to fix the problem and return the employee back to normal operation.

The second goal is only to support the third goal, so let's go there next. All exception processes must have a component to prevent exceptions in the future.

The Help Desk ticket process must support the prevention of future tickets. A manufacturing scrap process must support the prevention of future scrap. A customer complaint process must support the prevention of future customer complaints.

The owner of the process must understand this part of the process. Which brings us to the next part of this section: managing business processes.

All business processes need a process owner. This isn't necessarily the person who executes the process. This is the person who decides and documents how the process should be performed. While the process owner should gather input from other people, there can only be one process owner.

The process owner maintains the definition of the process. What steps are in the process? Who does those steps? What inputs are needed? What outputs are created? Is it well integrated with the upstream and downstream processes? What exception processes are needed?

This is very different from performing the process. The process owner for the employee onboarding process needs to be concerned with what steps are in the process. They think about what kinds of employees are being onboarded. For example, which groups need access to which systems, what equipment needs to be set up for different types of employees, or what job roles get which types of permissions?

The people *executing* the new employee process care only about the specific employee they are onboarding. For example, if Leland is starting next week, the Help Desk follows the process to create specific accounts, provide equipment, and assign permissions that Leland needs. Those executing the process can suggest improvements, but only the process owner can decide to implement those changes.

The owner must also monitor the process to make sure that it is operating properly. Is it working efficiently? Is it working correctly? How many exceptions are being created? Defining a small, but effective set of metrics is important here.

Keep the following points in mind when you think about metrics:

- Fewer is always better. Start with one or two metrics. Don't add more until you are monitoring and effectively using those.

- Collecting metrics has a cost. Don't underestimate this. Make intentional decisions about this cost.

- Track metrics over both short term and long term. Long term shows historical trends and improvements. Short term shows you what is happening right now and allows for quick correction.

- Every metric has a downside. What you measure is what you get. If you measure Help Desk only for time-to-close, people may rush tickets and quality may suffer. Measure only for quality and time-to-close may suffer. Consider groups of metrics that balance each other out.

The final responsibility of the process owner is to improve the process. The people doing the work will have ideas to be more efficient. The upstream and downstream processes may want different inputs and outputs. Business needs may require additional process steps. The process owner collects, prioritizes, and implements the improvement ideas.

One concern you will need to be aware of is local improvement versus overall processes. All processes fit together into a larger process. If each owner is looking to make local improvements in their process, is someone looking at the bigger picture? Sometimes making one process very efficient may make the larger organization less efficient. In systems theory, local optimization is good, but has the risk of hurting global optimization.

Or to put it more simply, sometimes one group has to do extra work that allows a downstream process to be more efficient. Think of customer setup or order entry that performs extra steps to make downstream processes more efficient. These extra steps slow down order entry, which may make the customer wait just a bit longer, but it makes production better. These tradeoffs can be hard to spot if process owners aren't talking.

Implementing process improvements is where IT earns its paycheck. As more business processes become dependent on computers and as more organizations drive for improvements, there is more work that needs to be done in the IT department.

You and your team are enablers of change. Any request that comes in is part of a business process that needs improving. Sometimes, such as with infrastructure changes, the improvement may be across multiple processes. Most of the time, the improvement will be for a single process.

As you look at the change requests that come into IT, keep in mind the following:

- What business process is being improved?
- Is the business owner involved?
- How does this fit into the list of improvements the process owner wants to implement?
- What process metrics will be improved?

One result of all this is your team will know business processes better than most everyone else in the organization. Sure, each department will know a few processes deeper, but as experience builds in your team, they will know all the inputs/outputs and improvements goals across all processes.

Managing The Work

The work the IT department does falls into two categories: (1) keeping the organization running, and (2) improving the organization. While much of IT's activity happens behind the scenes, it is important for the rest of the organization to understand how we organize the work. Not everyone will care, but the organization's management should have a clear understanding of how this works.

Keeping the organization running primarily consists of the Help Desk and a few regular tasks. Help Desk work is primarily fixing broken technology for employees. The regular tasks might be things like verifying backups are working, performing background tasks for financial cost rolls, or monitoring security logs. Remember the monitoring tools I mentioned earlier? Those are watching all of your systems, ready to alert you if something goes wrong.

Improving the organization will almost always require the implementation of new or improved functionality. This can be anything from improving network speeds, adding more storage, writing a new application, or scripting out a new workflow.

Sometimes the work takes a few hours. Sometimes the work takes a year or two.

How do we manage the work to best help the organization?

Each organization uses different terminology, so don't worry if the terms below differ from what you are used to. In addition, various standards, such as ITIL or COBIT, may use different terminology. The concepts are still the same. I use this grouping of the work because the prioritization is very different for each.

The four types of work that IT does are

1. Help Desk tickets—fixing broken technology
2. Service Requests—standard changes
3. Change Requests—custom changes
4. Projects—larger efforts that require specific management techniques.

Let's look at how to manage each of these types of IT work.

Help Desk Tickets

Help Desk tickets can come in via email, text, phone calls, automated alerts, and people walking in. There are many ticketing management systems on the market, so hopefully, your organization has one in place. If not, get one. These ticketing systems help your team keep track of all the tickets without dropping any. They can also provide satisfaction surveys, which is a likely metric.

The ticketing system provides the tracking mechanism. Your Help Desk will prioritize using first-in-first-out (FIFO) but will adjust the priority based on the severity of the problem (the risk management foundation we talked about). If it affects a large group of people, it is a higher priority. If it prevents the organization from directly serving the customer, for example, by preventing the shipping of a product, it is a top priority.

While you may need to have conversations with your Help Desk folks about specific tickets, make sure that you have regular conversations about prioritization. Talk about what kinds of tickets need attention right away and what kinds of tickets can sit for a bit if needed. The more they can prioritize on their own, the better the Help Desk will perform.

The tickets that come in won't just be broken technology. They will also be requests for information or training, questions about how the systems work, or triggers for the other types of work. Tickets can also be questions which will require investigation to resolve.

Service Requests

Service Requests are standard changes. These requests come in frequently and vary only in the specifics. Examples include adding new employees, enabling VPN, providing a replacement computer, updating automated report distribution lists, and so forth.

Service Requests often have a form that users fill out to ensure consistent inputs. A standard process for each Service Request is used to ensure the process has the same results each time, regardless of which person is doing the work.

Defining success for service requests focuses on the areas of speed and quality. Being able to respond to these changes quickly is a significant benefit to the organization. If you can get notification of a new employee and have everything ready for them, including hardware, software, account setup, etc., the next day, the organization can move faster. The same point applies to installing an application, granting access to data, or getting a new mobile phone.

The less time the organization spends waiting for IT to make these changes, the better.

Prioritizing Service Requests is straightforward and typically uses FIFO. Since the goal is to do these efficiently, they shouldn't take much time.

> *The less time the organization spends waiting for IT to make these changes, the better.*

Change Requests

Change Requests are non-standard changes. These changes can apply anywhere in the IT technology space: improving the Wi-Fi in an area, updating an application, creating a new report, designing and implementing a new workflow for accounts receivable, and so forth.

Smaller than projects, Change Requests don't require much project-management overhead and can range from a few minutes to add a column in a report to a couple of months to create a new application.

These changes can come in from anywhere in the company and prioritization can be difficult. In fact, prioritizing Change Requests can be more contentious than any other type of IT work.

The various departments of the organization will want their Change Requests prioritized highest. You will end up balancing the needs of the departments against the needs of the entire organization.

This balancing will take place in one of two ways:

1. There is a committee from across the company that prioritizes all incoming change requests into one list. While this sounds ideal to some, keep in mind that this committee will only want to look at bigger change requests. They won't want to prioritize reports and other small changes. It will still fall on IT to prioritize those. IT will also require time and effort from the committee members to keep up with the prioritization process.

2. Each department will have a prioritized list of Change Requests and you and your team will work off the top of each list. This may seem like more work, but it puts

more control into IT's hands. I feel that this approach, with an honest effort to match the organization's priorities is the best way to go.

Remember when I said your most important job was to know the organization? Balancing multiple prioritized department lists is one place this is necessary. By knowing what is important to the entire organization, you can help your team prioritize Change Requests effectively. You won't be able to keep everyone happy, but you want to be able to say that, at any given time, IT is working on the most important Change Requests for the organization and have most of the leadership team agree with you.

> *By knowing what is important to the entire organization, you can help your team prioritize Change Requests effectively.*

Projects

In the world of IT work, projects are larger efforts where IT is handling the project management task. IT Projects are typically efforts like ERP upgrades, major IT infrastructure improvements, and new system installations where the company feels that IT leading the project is appropriate.

Typically, business process projects led by the organization will lead to Change Requests that IT can track and manage as discrete work elements. There is a gray area between projects and collections of Change Requests, so we need to use our judgment on what works best.

A successful project is one that comes in on time, on budget, and meets requirements. Easy to say, hard to do. The project management method used will vary from organization to organization. If there is a Project Management Office (PMO) we can follow their project management method. If not, then we are free to use whatever method we wish.

We typically prioritize projects at an organizational level as they involve more people and larger financial investments. The high-level priorities of the organization drive these.

However, IT-driven projects are harder to get scheduled because the value they provide rarely comes with a deadline. The network upgrade, for example, can be put off again, right? It isn't urgent, right? Until the network breaks and then it becomes urgent.

Many of these upgrade projects, while technically improvements, can best be considered maintenance on your car or furnace. You can wait until it breaks, or you can maintain it properly (upgrading as needed) and reduce the chance of a breakdown.

Chapter Five

PEOPLE

As a new IT leader, you get to lead a team of people. You may have had some experience leading a team in the past, or this may be the first time you have had this responsibility.

Managing people has been the hardest part of my job, and the most rewarding. It's difficult to manage a situation where someone is in the wrong position and changes need to be made. It's wonderful to see an employee grow into a new role, showing abilities they were unaware they had.

It's wonderful to see an employee grow into a new role, showing abilities they were unaware they had.

Your team is made up of people with personal lives, skills, quirks, hopes, dreams, foibles, and strengths. Real people that go home to real situations. They are not pieces on a chessboard. They are not mix and match toy blocks that can be rearranged at will or fit into any slot.

They won't have the same background you have. They won't know what you know. And vice versa. Each person can learn something from you. You can learn from each person.

People will disagree with you. They won't follow standard procedures. They will make mistakes. That's ok.

They will be smarter than you. They will figure out better ways to do things than you. They will understand technology better than you. That's also ok.

You will make mistakes with people, you will assign a task to someone who will fail, and you will miss some signals of an unhappy employee and be surprised when they leave. You will struggle to connect with an employee. You will need to apologize for dropping a ball or accidentally putting someone in an awkward position.

You will make a great hire and watch that person succeed. You will help an employee through a difficult time. You will identify and nurture unexpected skills and watch a young employee grow in areas they didn't expect. You will identify and foster new leaders.

You will learn. You will grow.

You may never be as good a leader as you want to be. And you can always be a better leader than you are today.

I hope this won't be the only leadership book that you read. Talk to other leaders about books that inspired them. Poke around a bookstore to see what you find. Find a leader in your organization that you admire and use them as a sounding board. Take part in a mentorship program if your organization offers one.

In this chapter on managing people, I cover three topics that are important to new leaders. These apply to any leadership position, but since this is an IT leadership book, the examples and explanations will come from that direction.

The first section is about building on your team's strengths. Each person is good at certain things. As a leader, knowing each team member's strengths helps you arrange the work to get it all done.

Next, I will cover trust, specifically you trusting the team. People accomplish more when they know you trust them to do a good job.

I finish the chapter with a section about mistakes. We all make them, some big, some small. This is a fact that we can't change. What we can change is how we respond when we make a mistake. Taking responsibility, making amends, and communicating clearly won't erase the mistake, but it will affect how others respond to it and to you.

Even though I am near the end of my career, I am still learning how to better manage people. I encourage you to keep learning throughout your career.

Build on Strengths

Everyone has things they are good at. Sometimes it comes naturally, and they have a talent for a skill, task, or effort. Sometimes there is a passion that drives the person forward, continually learning and improving. These strengths are a key to getting the most from the team.

In the book I mentioned earlier, *First, Break All the Rules*, the authors present research that shows that leveraging employee's strengths leads to higher performance and better engagement. I highly recommend this book and the follow-up *Now, Discover Your Strengths* (Marcus Buckingham and Donald O. Clifton).

What does it mean to build on strengths?

The first step is to identify them. This can be a formal tool like *StrengthsFinder* (Gallup Press). This tool ranks your strengths from a list of generic strengths. Do this for yourself and for each member of your team.

You can, and should, also get to know them well enough to know what they are good at. Here is an example: At a company I used to work at, we had an ERP system that would have a data glitch once in a while. These problems often originated in our data, but required a lot of digging to find the problem. Help Desk personnel would go back and forth with the end users trying to track down the problem.

On rare occasions, one of the team, Mae, would get pulled into the bad data glitches. She would dive in and figure out the answer quickly. Like a scuba diver surfacing after finding buried treasure, she would triumphantly emerge from her office with the solution and an enormous smile on her face. But it wasn't officially part of her job, so the Help Desk didn't send them to Mae often.

After a few conversations with the team, I realized not only was Mae good at solving these problems; she was faster than anyone else, better at identifying root cause, and most importantly, she loved doing it. Finding and resolving that type of problem was very satisfying for her.

So, I made the decision that this class of problem was always to go straight to Mae, bypassing the normal help desk process. As a team, we solved this class of problem faster. Mae enjoyed her job more, and the problems became rarer.

Mae had a strength and putting it to use was beneficial to the company, the team, and of course, Mae.

Talk to your team and find out what they like doing or what makes them feel productive. Ask them to remember a good day at work, when they headed home feeling good and eager to get back the next day; and to remember what specifically made them feel that way.

Find a way to have them do more of that.

Sometimes it is vague, and you have to dig. Statements like "I like to solve problems" and "I like to help people" always have specifics behind them. Ask more questions.

Sometimes you have an employee that says they never have a good day. Then you have to dig harder or have a conversation about job fit.

You will also learn their strengths by watching them over time. Which tasks do they complete quickly or seek out? Which tasks do they jump into right away?

Look to assign tasks to leverage the strengths of the team. As with Mae in the story above, adjusting responsibilities to leverage strengths can help everyone.

Of course, unless you are really lucky, your team's strengths will not match all the work that needs to be done. I've never been lucky like that. There will always be tasks that aren't very much fun for anyone. However, the more often people are doing the things they enjoy, the more they are willing to do the less-fun work once in a while.

> *The more often people are doing the things they enjoy, the more they are willing to do the less-fun work once in a while.*

It isn't possible for any of us to spend every day only doing things that make us feel awesome. That's why they call it work. Every job has parts of it that don't thrill us, and maybe even some parts that we actively dislike.

But if we understand what parts make each person feel better about themselves and their job, we can make changes—some subtle, some overt—to leverage their strengths. This results in a stronger department and an increase in job satisfaction and engagement.

Trust Your Team

One of the most important aspects of our jobs is trust. We make decisions every day that are influenced by the level of trust we have in our co-workers. Trust in our supervisor influences our choices in activities and even whether to stay in the job.

There is an aspect of trust that isn't talked about as much as the others.

How much do you, as a leader, trust your team?

Most of us, hopefully, will answer, "a lot" or "very much." We believe we trust our team to do the work.

Some of us might have some issues to work on. However, while there are a few employees that are truly not trustworthy (leading to a conversation about job performance), we can generally trust people on our teams.

The question is: do our actions show that trust? Or to put it another way: do our employees feel we trust them?

Micromanagers, of course, demonstrate they do not trust their team by constantly checking in and dictating the specific details of how to do their job. The employee becomes afraid of making mistakes and starts checking in with their manager each and every step of the way.

A classic Harvard Business Review article by William Oncken Jr. and Donald L. Wass, "Management Time: Who's Got the Monkey?" is a great article about effective delegation. It is a quick read, but very helpful in framing up how we interact with our team. Monkeys are the various tasks and problems our employees face. The monkey represents the responsibility for the task. Task owners have to feed the monkey(s) on their shoulder with actions and communication.

As leaders, we often (unintentionally) encourage monkeys to jump from the employee's shoulder to our shoulder.

As leaders, we often (unintentionally) encourage monkeys to jump from the employee's shoulder to our shoulder. This requires us to do the care and feeding of the monkey.

I'm not talking about the cute little monkeys that scamper about at the zoo and sit sweetly looking at us. I'm talking about the aggressive, rip-the-backpack-of-food-from-our-hands-and-run-kind. If you have ever visited Gibraltar, you know the kinds of monkeys I'm talking about. You don't want them sitting on your shoulders.

We transfer monkeys to our own shoulder in very subtle ways, and often with the best of intentions. Anytime we say, "Let me check into that" or "Send me an email about it," we have allowed the monkey to jump from the employee's shoulders to ours. We now have a brand new, hungry monkey to care for. How many times do we do this in a day or week?

The point of the article is about managing our time. It assumes that employees want to get rid of all their monkeys. Written in a time when the primary management style was command and control, the word *trust* doesn't appear in the article. But looking at it through the lens of today's management styles, it is clear the authors are talking about trusting your team to take care of their own monkeys. Stephen Covey points this out in an afterward written to accompany the article reprints.

If you leave the monkey on your employee's shoulder, you show you trust them to take care of it. They may have questions or want advice, but leaving it with them communicates your trust. I don't think it hurts to point it out specifically. "I trust you to take care of this" is a powerful message.

Here is a simple test for how much you trust your employees. When they are working on a task that you know how to do, how do you react when they handle it a different way? How do you respond when they set up the project plan differently? Or analyze risk differently? Or interact with the rest of the business in a way that you wouldn't?

Do you keep your mouth shut or do you speak up?

Obviously, you need to speak up once in a while. Equally obviously, there is more than one way to do the same task. If they get the results, isn't that what matters? You are trusting them to get the job done, not to do it exactly as you would have done it.

Spend your time on the important matters such as prioritization and quality of work. Set the goals and expectations and let the employees get there in their own way.

By trusting them to meet the goals and expectations, you will find that the entire team will get more accomplished.

Mistakes Happen—what matters is what happens next

Imagine two scenarios:

First, we are at a restaurant. Scanning the menu, we see lots of great options. It's hard to decide. But finally, we do. We put our order in and sit back, mouth watering in anticipation. Finally, it arrives. And it's wrong. We wanted french fries and got brussels sprouts. Or vice versa.

Either way, it disappoints us. When we point it out, the restaurant is very apologetic, brings out new food and takes something off the bill.

Second scenario. Same restaurant. Same menu. And we once again get the Brussels sprouts. Sigh. This time, the restaurant suggests that we really do want the brussels sprouts because they are superb. They seem reluctant to fix the problem. Finally, they bring out a small plate of fries, giving the impression that it is a big hassle. And make no change to the bill.

Leaving aside the brutal reality of restaurant economics, the first scenario is better. The restaurant made a mistake, but they acknowledged it and fixed it quickly.

We all have stories like this: a car takes too long to get repaired, a movie theater charges an extra ticket on the credit card, or a vendor drops the ball on a task handoff. A mistake is made and then handled. Sometimes we discover it. Sometimes, even better, the vendor discovers it and tells us about it. "I'm sorry, but it will take a day longer to get your car done. We ordered the wrong part. We discovered it, ordered the correct part, and we have taken 5% off your bill for the delay."

When someone acknowledges their mistakes and works to make amends, we feel differently about them. Sometimes, these situations connect us more closely to a vendor because we have now seen how they do business and what level of integrity they have. Everybody makes mistakes, some handle it better than others.

At our work in the IT department, we are the provider. We are the restaurant, the auto repair shop, the movie theater. While we shouldn't call our co-workers *customers*, we must build a strong customer service mentality. We will make mistakes. How we deal with them is the important part.

> We will make mistakes. How we deal with them is the important part.

There are two parts to "dealing with" a mistake: Acknowledgment and Improving.

Acknowledgment

Acknowledging mistakes is important. It lets the other person know we are transparent in how things are working. They know something is wrong, so don't hide it.

If we drop the ball on something, apologize. Owning the mistake makes it clear that we are not trying to cover things up.

Now there is a gray area between trumpeting our team's mistakes from the tallest tower and hiding them. We will make mistakes we don't need to broadcast outside the people involved. Broadcasting differs from acknowledging them. Acknowledging them to those directly involved is key here.

Having a reputation for not owning up to mistakes will undermine our credibility in the organization. Much better to have a reputation for owning and fixing our mistakes.

Acknowledging a mistake allows everyone to move on. When there are arguments about whom to blame, the entire organization suffers.

Improving

We can't really give a $10 coupon when IT makes a mistake. We can't give them a meal at half price. But we can reduce the chance of making that mistake again. It isn't possible to prevent all future mistakes, but communicating that we are working to reduce mistakes makes a lot of difference.

Internally, the focus should be on the future. Do we need to prevent this mistake from happening? Or do we need to reduce the possibility that it will happen? Risk analysis and mitigation can help here.

Mistakes come from the process more than the person: a process that doesn't take a certain situation into account, or a person we haven't trained sufficiently. That doesn't mean we don't individually mess up, but it means that improving the process may be more beneficial than placing blame on a person.

Mistakes can be teaching moments. Often, a self-driven person will see the mistake they made and come up with a suitable response to reduce the chance of it happening in the future. Sometimes, though, it is helpful to talk about the bigger picture behind the problem.

For example, if they dropped the ball on a task because they had too many active tasks at once, the conversation shouldn't be about dropping the ball, but about how to better manage open tasks and the need to focus and finish to avoid these kinds of problems.

Yes, sometimes an employee makes too many mistakes, and we need to address a mismatch between the needs of the job and the skills. But this isn't a common thing.

It is far more common that we all make mistakes. When they happen, we need to acknowledge them, learn from them, and move on.

CHAPTER SIX

TECHNOLOGY

You are in IT because you like working with technology. Checking out a new data analysis tool, adding a programming language to your skill set, connecting your phone to almost anything. The thrill of new technology is real for many of us.

You like making technology useful for others.

In your new leadership role, you will make decisions about how your organization will use that technology. You have to balance your "This is so cool!" response with the more important "Would the organization benefit from this technology?" question.

This chapter will not contain commentary on specific technology. Instead, I will cover a few topics that will help you think about technology.

The first topic is to understand the portfolio of technology currently in place. This portfolio will probably be larger than you think. I'll talk a bit about three tools to help you keep this information organized.

Vendors will provide all your technology. I cover how to work with these vendors and make sure both of you are successful.

You will make tradeoffs on Technical Debt frequently. Is it worth putting in the extra work to completely remove an old technology? Or do the pressures of the current situation require that you push that issue down the road to deal with in the future? This section of the chapter will help you think about Technical Debt.

I end the chapter with a discussion about security. This is a critical part of how you approach the job. Again, I won't discuss specific technology because it changes too fast. Instead, I will focus on how to evaluate the technologies and apply them to a comprehensive security approach.

Technical Portfolio

When I bought my first house, a wise person told me I should consider myself a temporary caretaker and keep the house well maintained while I lived there. If possible, I should try to sell the house in better shape than when I bought it. Whether I stayed in the house for two years or fifty years, new owners would eventually live there and the decisions and actions I took would directly affect their lives. Some parts, like painting and curtains, are easy to change. Some parts, like the plumbing, electrical, or the furnace, would last for years and I needed to balance my financials with the long term when I made changes.

If the house is new, everything is shiny and fresh and there isn't much maintenance. I have never lived in a brand-new house, but I have lived in old houses. I lived in a house built in 1971, one built in 1888, and several in between. These houses had a motley collection of heating, electrical, plumbing, and other systems. Prior owners had replaced or upgraded everything at least once.

We have a responsibility to leave the organization in better shape than we found it, regardless of whether everything is shiny and fresh or a haphazard mix of old and new.

When we step into the IT leadership role at a company, it is like buying a house. We are caretakers in a chain of caretakers. We have a responsibility to leave the organization in better shape than we found it, regardless of whether everything is shiny and fresh or a haphazard mix of old and new.

If you don't have the mindset of leaving things better than you found them, I'm not sure that IT Leader is the right job for you.

Your technology portfolio is the collection of all purchased and built technologies that run the organization's information systems. Everything from the operating systems we use to the network infrastructure to that one weird app used to do some unique task. The technology portfolio also includes the consumer technology that sneaks in and around our company regardless of our attempts to manage it.

Consider a sailing race. Imagine a large sailing ship with lots of sails and a sizable crew. We might think of a majestic sailing ship from days of old, or we might think of a sleek yacht. Doesn't matter. If it has sails, it is in the race.

This race isn't for a certain distance or certain time. This is a permanent race. It never stops and has been going on for years.

Over time, everything changes. Crew members come and go. Some have been sailing for years, some are new to the game. New competitors join and old competitors drop out. The rules constantly change. There is no finish line, but there are rewards for being the fastest. New technologies to enable greater speeds are coming out regularly.

But the race never stops. There are no breaks from the race, so we can't stop for weeks at a time to swap out major components like the hull or sails. We need to figure out how to change them while continuing to race.

And, of course, at some point, some bright person comes up with the idea of adding an engine to the ship and completely changes the race. New competitors enter that have only engines and no sails. The race has transformed, and we must change to stay competitive—while we are still racing.

We are in charge of the physical ship. Others are in charge of the crew, giving orders, figuring out destinations, etc.

In our world, we are in charge of the technical portfolio. Others are in charge of the people, processes, finances, markets, selling, etc. The race never takes a break, and we need to maintain (and sometimes replace) every part of the technology portfolio over time.

Whew! Sounds daunting, doesn't it?

Fortunately, you can start small and build. You will never know as much about the portfolio as you want, but you can make a good start by using a few simple tools:

1. Applications List
2. High-level network diagram
3. Major Interfaces list

Let's look at each of these.

Keeping an application list will help you and your team understand how much software you are managing. To create your application list, capture the following information for each piece of software:

- Name
- Vendor
- Installed Version
- Current Version
- User Information (number, scope, departments, names, etc.)
- Maintenance Information (costs, programs, expiration dates, etc.)
- Desktop, web, or software-as-a-service (Saas)
- Notes for information that doesn't fit in the other fields

You will have some other ideas as you build this list. Once the list exists, you will find all sorts of uses for it.

Keep the list simple and make sure you and your team keep it updated. You will need to make some judgements on what to include. For example, I don't track operating system versions, but some people do.

The number of entries in this list will surprise you. There will be a lot of little applications that are used by one or two people. Your own

IT department probably has a dozen or two applications that no other department uses.

Look for places where you can consolidate multiple applications with a single application. Look for unused applications. Your team should activity manage this list to meet the organization's functional and financial needs.

A quick note about software maintenance. There are two schools of thought about buying maintenance from vendors. The first is "keep maintenance on it or kill it." This approach understands that all software gets old and problematic. If your organization is using it, it is worth buying maintenance. The other approach is "buy maintenance for the important applications, everything else changes too fast to waste money on maintenance." This approach saves money and effort. I lean more towards the first approach, but organizations have been successful with the second.

Your next tool, the network diagram, is helpful for understanding the size and scope of the technology portfolio. A good network diagram will show

- Physical locations (buildings, server rooms, network equipment locations)
- Outside network connections and vendors (with support contact information)
- Security components and control points
- Major VLANs
- Wired & wireless networks
- DNS & DHCP servers

Your infrastructure team will create and maintain this diagram and have their own opinion on what it should contain. Keeping the diagram up to date is critical. As with the application list, a simple list kept up to date is better than a complex list that is stale.

The network list is useful during troubleshooting outages or weird network behavior. New IT employees can use it to get a quick overview of the network. It is a great tool for planning maintenance and upgrades, as well as implementing failover strategies.

The last tool is the major interfaces list. Some applications on your list will interface with each other. There is likely a major system like an ERP or central client system that has many interfaces to other applications or databases. There may be a data warehouse system, external customer systems, or supplier systems that have interfaces as well.

This list of interfaces would have the following information:

- Source system
- Connecting system
- Type of interface (live, synchronous, transfer, manual)
- Timing information (if not live)
- Interface description
- Business purpose
- Consequences of interface failure

One use of this list is to make sure there is something in place to monitor each interface. All interfaces fail at some point. In fact, doing a short risk assessment of each interface will show you which interfaces may need work to reduce the likelihood or severity of failure.

This list will also be useful during upgrades of major systems. For example, when you are upgrading your ERP system, this list will give you the outline for your interface test plan.

Understanding your portfolio clearly will identify IT projects that need to be completed. These projects need to be woven in with the other organization projects. By staying on top of your portfolio and strategically scheduling the upgrades, you can avoid situations where you have to drop other work to urgently upgrade a problematic component of your system.

Vendors

Vendors are external resources that, in exchange for money, will provide your organization with products and services, or contractors and consultants (people). Most IT teams use both types.

Identify your vendors and understand what they are providing to your organization. Look for vendors that provide similar products. Look for vendors that you haven't done business with in a while.

As I mentioned earlier, you can divide the vendors that your organization uses into strategic and transactional. Transactional vendors are ones from which you simply buy a product or service, and you are comfortable switching between vendors to get a better price. Large distributors and online purchases fall into this category.

Strategic vendors are ones you build your department on. There will usually be a few strategic software companies that provide critical software, like operating systems, security, or central business applications. You might have several strategic consulting/contracting vendors that provide needed unique expertise.

Most of the information in this section refers to your strategic vendors. Pay attention to them and make sure both you and the vendor maintain the relationship.

The rest of this section will cover rules and guidelines for managing vendors. While every vendor is unique, there are some common factors that you can use to your benefit.

Know how they make money

Vendors are in business to make money. They will need to be profitable on your business or else they will walk away. Knowing how they make their money helps you understand what financially motivates them.

While this may be easy with vendors that sell a distinct product, it isn't always clear for some. Cloud vendors can have other sources of revenue (selling your data) that are hard to discover. If a product vendor offers a cloud version, they will have additional costs they need to recover from customers like you.

Knowing where they make money will allow you to negotiate better. Vendors likely won't budge in those areas but will be more flexible in other areas.

For example, consulting companies need to keep their staff fully billable to make sure they can pay their employee's salaries and make a profit. They care about predictability of billable hours and start/end dates of projects. If you can meet those needs, you can better negotiate other things like asking for specific people or a lower rate for situations where their staff needs to learn something new to help you.

Stay in the vendor's sweet spot

In sports where an object is used to hit a ball, there is usually an area of the object that is the best place to strike. Think of the barrel of a baseball bat, the face of a golf club, or the middle of a tennis racket. We call this the sweet spot, the place to get the most out of the swing.

Vendors have sweet spots. Strengths where you can get the most out of them. Where they can help your company the most for the money spent.

For example, a consulting business may have teams of people who can do web and database development, but only one or two people who can do user interface design. A vendor may have a successful primary product line and a new secondary product line. One product is established and solid, the other is new and won't be fully developed.

Learn what the vendor's sweet spot is, and stay in it.

Learn what the vendor's sweet spot is and stay in it. They will have a strong experience in their sweet spot. They will have multiple people and a culture to support continued excellence in that area.

If you are outside the vendor's sweet spot, you risk getting less than ideal support or having a product abandoned.

Be a good customer

The best vendor/customer relationships are win/win. You get products, services, and people that meet your organization's needs, and the vendor makes a profit and can invest in the business to grow and improve.

There is a school of thought that approaches vendors as a competition. That implies that every relationship has a winner and a loser. Negotiations with the vendor are to extract every penny from the deal and get the most value for your organization.

It is hard to argue with this approach. We all want to get the most value for our company. But this is a short-term/long-term concern. It works fine for transactional vendors. Strategic vendors require a longer-term relationship.

This is especially true of consulting/contracting companies that provide people to help your organization.

In my experience, developing a good relationship—that is, being a good customer—can get you access to better people and put you higher in the inevitable priority list of customers they keep.

Early in my leadership career, I was working with a vendor for database personnel. We had various projects and ongoing functions and had used a variety of their staff. I worked with them to make sure that it was a win/win. I would be flexible on project start dates. We were willing to make a commitment for longer term ongoing efforts.

This paid off when a sudden change in our business situation required us to make a large change very quickly. Our existing, positive relationship with the vendor motivated them to shuffle around staff with their other customers and got us good people very quickly.

Maybe we would have been able to find an overall cheaper vendor or maybe we could have constantly squeezed the vendor to get the absolutely lowest rate. However, the financial benefit to my organization of completing the sudden change quickly was far greater than any savings I could have realized.

Protect Both Parties

Your organization has information that you don't want made public. Trade secrets, patents, internal processes, private information are a few examples. Use bi-directional Non-disclosure Agreements (NDA) for all strategic vendors. Some vendors still have single-direction NDAs where you have to protect their information, but they don't have to protect yours. Fortunately, these seem to be disappearing. Your organization probably has a template for this.

Time & Materials Contracts

Time & Materials (T&M) contracts are better than fixed bid. T&M refers to agreements where we pay the vendor by the hour and for any expenses, typically for travel. Fixed Bid refers to a fixed amount of money paid for a defined set of work.

The following table summarizes the pros and cons of each option.

I prefer T&M agreements. You can get started faster, you pay for only the work performed, and if situations change, you can stop or take the project in a different direction more easily.

	Pros	Cons
Time & Materials (T&M)	• Payment matches work performed. • Easier to adjust to changes as the projects move along. • Faster to get started because you don't need to have everything figured out. • More flexibility if the project needs to change or pause due to business changes. • Invoices typically contain details about the work performed.	• Ill-defined projects can lead to cost overruns. • Requires more planning and tracking.
Fixed Bid	• You know the final cost when you start, presuming no changes. • You won't have to pay more if the vendor underestimated the project.	• Changes require more paperwork and often result in the final cost changing. • Slower to get started because you must document every requirement before the vendor can provide a quote. • If the vendor overestimated the work, you won't get any financial benefit. • If the vendor underestimated the work, the vendor may change their behavior to reduce their costs and that may not be good for you.

Build Deeper Technical Expertise

Use vendors for deep expertise in technical areas. Consider a large software system at the center of your business, for example, an ERP system. Your team has some level of knowledge of the system, but there are likely areas they don't know as deeply as a certain project or change request may require. Or perhaps the business wants to use a part of the system not used before.

Having a consulting company (or two!) that has deep knowledge ready to go allows your IT department to respond faster. Once you have a working relationship with them, consider setting up a pool of open hours. Have your team use these hours for questions or short research as needed.

I typically set it up for 16-40 hours T&M with no specific statement of work to be performed other than "questions and research as requested." I then tell my staff that they can contact the vendor if they need access to that deeper knowledge. We only get billed if the hours are used.

The biggest benefit is that your team member and the vendor don't need to worry about paperwork and billing. Your team moves faster. The vendor gets paid. Everyone wins.

Technical Debt

I have a set of shelves down in my basement laundry room. I am very good at ignoring the shelves as they are on the opposite wall from the washer and dryer.

On these shelves are a variety of boxes and bins and loose items. Special tools I rarely use, light bulbs, spare parts left over from prior house projects. Some things that I will certainly need in the future, some that I might need, and some that I will never need and really should throw away but, you know, I haven't done that yet.

You may not have a set of shelves like mine, but you almost certainly have a junk drawer in the kitchen. I do. Everyone seems to have a junk drawer. Like the shelves in the basement, there are a number of things in there that should probably be tossed or donated.

Technical Debt is the equivalent of our kitchen junk drawer—unused software, hardware, configuration settings, and data that sit around on your network or server room or storage rooms.

Technical Debt is the equivalent of our kitchen junk drawer or my shelves in the basement—unused software, hardware, configuration settings, and data that sit around on your network or server room or storage rooms. No longer used, but still hanging around.

Unfortunately, the consequences of Technical Debt are worse than our junk drawers. The only problem the useless stuff in our junk drawers causes is perhaps it takes longer to find something we are looking for. While Technical Debt certainly causes that problem, there are worse problems that can trip us up in the future.

This is all compounded by the fact that Technical Debt is like Schrodinger's Cat as it may or may not be there. Sometimes it causes problems in a few months or years, sometimes it never causes problems.

Let's look at some examples of technical debt. Note that these situations actually happened to me or my peers:

- A server with old software is left up and running "until we don't need it." That server has some background jobs that run against some other production servers. Staff's memory of this server, and the background jobs, fades over time. One day, the server loses its mind and runs all the background jobs constantly. The jobs all hit the other production servers and bring them to their knees, requiring a reboot of production. It wasn't until the second time this happened that I, er, my peer, figured out the cause.

- DHCP ranges are not kept up to date and accurate. Someone changes the rules on a range and causes a problem with a printer that takes a day to diagnose. This particular printer was used to print labels for manufacturing so we couldn't ship product that day.

- We didn't get around to updating the operating system after the last application release like we planned. A few years later, we can't update the phone system because we can't update the active directory version because we have old versions of the operating system hanging around. While they aren't usually this bad, these chains of causalities are common in Technical Debt.

- An old database was kept around "just in case." A few years later, someone reports their spreadsheet isn't working right. After much digging, we discovered the spreadsheets looked at both the new and old databases. The help desk technician and business analyst looking into it weren't even employed at the company when the old database was in place, so it didn't even cross their mind as a possibility. Two days of wasted time because we didn't shut down the old database.

- An old application was left up and running, only accessed by "a few." The term *few* turned out to be several dozen people that had needed access to the old system. Even though they had been trained in the new system, they liked the old system better, so they kept working there. There was current data in both systems that needed to be reconciled. A week of wasted time.

- We have all seen messy cable racks, right? That is classic Technical Debt. Paid every time we need to trace a cable to solve a problem.

- Old computers that had been retired were kept in a storage closet, instead of being disposed of properly. An industrious intern, chartered with upgrading the operating system for the company, found them, and spent a week upgrading old computers unnecessarily.

Technical Debt also shows up in the assumptions we make along the way. Some Technical Debt is never a problem. Some of it blows up spectacularly. Some assumptions we make are fine. Others aren't. Here are some examples:

- A small company doesn't put a Country field into their addresses because they have no plans to be international. Until five successful years later, when they do.

- In the 1970s, everyone knew they would replace their software by the year 2000, so two digits for the year were fine. Until it wasn't.

- A developer uses an undocumented feature in the underlying operating system that works fine. Until it doesn't.

- The database developer writes code that only works with on-premise databases because there are no plans to move this critical database to the cloud. Until there are.

How do you prevent Technical Debt? In the Foundations chapter, we talked about Focus & Finish. Much of the attention was on the "focus" part; making sure that you and your team have a small number of active tasks. The "finish" part means completing the tasks with everything that needs to be done.

Often these tasks, say rolling out a new application, have tasks that need to be completed at the end. Finishing the task means cleaning up all the old files, setting, servers, and source code from the old application. It means shutting down the old system completely. It means removing security groups that controlled the old system.

A frequent contributor to Technical Debt is the phrase "let's leave it up for a while just in case." This is exactly the same as "I'll throw it in the junk drawer in case I need it in the future."

But as we have seen, doing this in the IT world causes many more problems than our junk drawer.

As we get near the end of a task, this cleanup is often the boring stuff. Like at home, the next thing needs our attention, and the cleanup doesn't happen as it should. Unlike at home, we pay a higher price for Technical Debt than we do a messy junk drawer.

Make sure to give your team time at the end to cleanup appropriately. "Done" doesn't mean when the code is pushed into production, it means when all the old stuff is retired. Point out when problems are caused by old stuff that didn't get cleaned up. Help the team understand that the time spent removing Technical Debt is time spent investing in the future.

Of course, checking assumptions is important.

My (mostly) joke to my development team is that you should program in only three numbers: zero, one, and infinity. Anything else is a landmine waiting to go off. Infinity, of course, is not feasible in computer systems, but at least it gets the conversation to larger numbers than initially expected and that has prevented problems down the road.

Workflow processes are another place where assumptions can bite you down the road. Document the assumptions in a place everyone knows about. Otherwise, it will be forgotten until it causes a problem.

The two reasons most often given for accepting some level of Technical Debt are, unfortunately, the two most valid: time and money. The standard joke is "We don't

"We don't have time to fix it today, but we will make time to fix it tomorrow."

have time to fix it today, but we will make time to fix it tomorrow." The unfortunate reality is that this will be true for any IT organization at some level.

The fight against Technical Debt is constant. We will make tradeoffs and accept risks daily. Some will turn out wrong and others will be right. If we don't work to reduce Technical Debt, we will pay for it with our future time.

Keep fighting!

Security

Stories of security breaches, privacy issues, stolen passwords, and crippling computer attacks have become common. There is a technological arms race between attackers and protectors. The attacks are becoming more sophisticated and more intentional. The products and services to protect your organization are becoming more complicated.

You are likely already familiar with all of this.

You have experienced security systems at your work either as a user or because you worked on them. Now that you are in a leadership position, you have more of a responsibility to protect the organization.

Imagine your organization is a submerged navy submarine, and the water represents the bad actors trying to get in. Submarines have two hulls to withstand the outside pressure. However, if you look at submarine design, it doesn't assume the hulls will successfully keep all water out all the time. Even with two hulls, they assume water will still get in. There are design features to deal with the water that will come in: watertight bulkheads, drains, pumps and more.

But a navy doesn't stop there. It trains everyone on the submarine. Intensely. Following processes and safety techniques is critical to ensuring the safety of all on board.

Your organization needs a similar approach. There must be a strong perimeter, probably more than one. You must assume the bad actors will get in and have internal tools in place to fight them. You must have a training and awareness program in place to emphasize the seriousness of the situation.

You must assume the bad actors will get in and have internal tools in place to fight them.

The concept of *zero-trust* is good for you to learn. Zero-trust says that no person, device, or application should be trusted by default, even after authentication. Read several articles as people have different spins on the topic.

Security, at its core, is about risk reduction (see "Risk Management" on page 62). You can never ensure your company will be 100% secure. You won't be able to spend an unlimited amount of money on security. In fact, the organization will not spend, indeed can't afford, the money you think necessary. This tension exists in every IT department and yours will be no different. Reduce the biggest risks and spend the money wisely.

The bad actors are constantly improving their weapons and the security companies are improving products to provide better defenses. Presume that you will change some part of your security program at least yearly.

This is all complicated by the fact your riskiest security problem is people. From the classic examples of people plugging in a USB drive they found in the parking lot to those that click on email links that download malware, people are often the weakest link.

To mitigate this, your security program must include an ongoing, and frequently updated, education and testing component. Employees won't be happy about it, but there really isn't a choice. A navy trains their people intensely to behave in a way that keeps water out. It is reasonable to expect your employees to spend a little time learning how to keep the bad actors out.

Security Considerations:

Improving security should be a constant effort

Set up a small security team that will create, maintain, and implement security improvements. You will provide them with budgetary guidance and determine how much time they should spend on it. I recommend having at least one security-improvement task active at all times, even if it is a small one like increasing awareness of the latest phishing attack.

Limit permissions

Limit permissions for accounts to only what is necessary to get the job done. Setting up a normal and admin account for IT personnel allows them to work in their normal account most of the time. When they need permissions, they log into their admin account, do the work, and log out.

Do you, personally, need elevated permissions? You are spending most of your time doing leader tasks (people, budgets, meetings, etc.) that don't require them. Reduce the potential impact of attacks on you (or mistakes you might make) by limiting your permissions.

Ability does not mean permission

Just because you and your team can see something, doesn't mean you should look. Permissions for backups and other system administrative tasks allow visibility into everything in the company. Departments like Human Resources and Finance get nervous with IT's ability to access everything. Keep this to a minimum and remind your team to always involve those departments before you access their information.

For example, you probably have internet access logs and other what-are-people-doing type of information. You and your team probably don't look at it unless there is a problem. You may not even have much logging turned on.

At some point, you or a team member will get approached by a supervisor in the company who has a concern about an employee. They feel the employee is spending too much time on the internet and they want the data to support that conclusion.

Don't give it to them.

Get HR involved. It is an employee performance problem, not an IT problem. If HR comes to you, great, give HR the information, not the supervisor.

Single Sign-On is good and bad

Single Sign-On (a.k.a. common authentication) is a double-edged sword. It will be a great convenience for your employees. Who wants to manage all those usernames and passwords for different systems? Unfortunately, it also means that if an attacker gets access to one account, they may have access to other accounts on other systems. Be aware of the tradeoff as you make the decisions that are best for your specific organization.

Monitoring

Set monitoring on all your security products to make sure they are operating properly. This is especially true of employees' computers. Just like regular inspections on a submarine, your team needs to be constantly vigilant to make sure all the pieces are in place and working properly.

Security is a hard problem and getting harder. Plan on adding or changing products regularly. Stay current on new techniques used to attack and to protect. Work with other managers to reinforce the idea that employees are part of the solution.

Luck, good or bad, plays a role in security. Proper preparation and diligence will allow you to reduce the dependency on luck.

In Closing

From the skills you need to be an I.T. Leader, to what you need to do in your first days, weeks, and months, to the concepts of Foundation, Business, People, and Technology, I have given you information that will help you succeed in your new IT leadership position.

There will be fun times and there will be not-so-fun times. The rollercoaster ride of leadership is not for the faint of heart.

Those that show up, work hard, learn fast, and have fun can succeed in this very demanding, and rewarding career.

Good Luck!

The I.T. Leader's First Days

Afterword

Thanks for reading this book! I hope you found it helpful. If you found it useful, head on over to The-It-Director.com and sign up for the newsletter to hear about upcoming books and events.

Over the years, I have mentored several new IT leaders. We had lots of discussions about the challenges they face and skills they should learn. This book came out of all those sessions.

Your leadership journey is unique to you. Your unique combination of abilities, interests, and experiences will shape the type of leader you are.

As a first-time IT leader, you will face challenges, dilemmas, and choices that you haven't faced before. This book will be part of your learning to be a great IT leader.

However, the learning isn't complete. The best leaders are the ones that are always learning.

My website, The-IT-Director.com, has resources for new and existing IT leaders. Wherever you are on your journey, you will find something helpful. There is even an "Ask The IT Director" section where you can send in questions.

REFERENCES & RECOMMENDATIONS

I mentioned several books and resources and have collected them here for your convenience. Go to The-IT-Director.com/FirstDays/Resources to also see this list.

1. *The I.T. Leaders' Handbook*, John A. Bredesen
2. The-IT-Director.com is a website targeting IT leaders of small-to-medium-sized organizations, typically $1M-$300M in revenue.
3. *First, Break All The Rules*, Marcus Buckingham & Curt Coffman
4. *Now, Discover Your Strengths*, Marcus Buckingham & Donald O. Clifton, Ph.D.
5. *StrengthsFinder 2.0*, Tom Rath
6. *The First 90 Days*, Michael Watkins
7. Part 1 of The Everyday Astronaut Elon Musk interview. In a video interview on Everyday Astronaut, a highly recommended YouTube channel for anyone interested in rockets and space travel, Elon Musk talks about organizations being cruise missiles instead of cannonballs. The three-part interview is well worth the watch, but the cruise missile comment comes in Part 3 at about 15:55.

Leadership books, like most self-help books, will have some good points and some points that don't resonate with you. That's ok. No leadership book, including this one, will be perfect. Take the concepts and ideas that make sense to you and leave the rest.

The books I list below look at leadership from a generic point of view. Any leader in any type of organization can find something helpful in each book.

- *The 7 Habits of Highly Effective People*, Stephen R. Covey
- *Gung Ho!*, Ken Blanchard & Sheldon Bowles
- *The New One Minute Manager*, Ken Blanchard & Spencer Johnson
- *Grit: The Power of Passion and Perseverance*, Angela Duckworth
- *The Five Dysfunctions of a Team*, Patrick Lencioni
- *Crucial Conversations*, Kerry Patterson, Joseph Grenny, Ron McMillan, & Al Switzler
- *Lean In*, Sheryl Sandberg
- *Who Moved My Cheese?*, Spencer Johnson
- *How To Win Friends and Influence People*, Dale Carnegie

QUOTES

9: Imagine your job is to fit as much as possible into the jar.

11: You control your devices, don't let them control you.

14: Your job requires that you be able to talk in both high- and low-level detail.

16: It's like trying to make a puzzle of a movie instead of a static picture.

19: In your position, you have access to more structured and unstructured data than anyone in the company.

22: The opinions of others are also important inputs for your decisions.

25: A good decision implemented well may be better than the best decision implemented poorly.

27: The type of meeting (status, decision, brainstorming, investigation, or negotiation) sets the tone and expected outcome of the meeting.

28: The first aspect of respecting people's time is to not invite them to meetings they don't need to be at.

31: What if you could come up to speed faster than people expect?

33: Schedule one-on-one meetings with the leadership team members and other key managers and individuals.

35: $$$$

37: The more the organization needs to change its business processes, the more work for IT, and therefore the bigger the IT budget will need to be.

41: As goes the infrastructure, so goes the organization.

44: Use the "minimum permissions needed" concept everywhere.

48: Opportunity cost refers to the cost of what isn't being worked on.

54: Continually taking small steps to improve yourself will result in large gains over the years.

54: The culture of the team affects everything, including CI, and therefore the improvements you can implement.

57: What did I do wrong? Two things: I didn't understand that change is hard, and I didn't listen to the users.

59: Have a very small number of active tasks and make sure that each one gets completed properly.

64: Monitoring security, applications, and processes are next steps which can really reduce the firefighting your team has to do.

67: Yes, your most important job is to look outside the IT department at the larger organization.

71: Not only do we need to understand these processes, but we must also understand the technology that enables them, so that we can improve them as the organization requires.

77: The less time the organization spends waiting for IT to make these changes, the better.

78: By knowing what is important to the entire organization, you can help your team prioritize Change Requests effectively.

80: It's wonderful to see an employee grow into a new role, showing abilities they were unaware they had.

83: The more often people are doing the things they enjoy, the more they are willing to do the less-fun work once in a while.

84: As leaders, we often (unintentionally) encourage monkeys to jump from the employee's shoulder to our shoulder.

86: We will make mistakes. How we deal with them is the important part.

90: We have a responsibility to leave the organization in better shape than we found it, regardless of whether everything is shiny and fresh or a haphazard mix of old and new.

96: Learn what the vendor's sweet spot is, and stay in it.

99: Technical Debt is the equivalent of our kitchen junk drawer—unused software, hardware, configuration settings, and data that sit around on your network or server room or storage rooms.

102: "We don't have time to fix it today, but we will make time to fix it tomorrow."

103: You must assume the bad actors will get in and have internal tools in place to fight them.

The I.T. Leader's First Days

Thanks

A book takes more than just the author to make it into a reality.

- Kristin Erlandsen is the word-whisperer who had to work overtime to smooth out awkward sentences and eliminate all my grammar errors. Alas, sometimes I am stubborn about my writing, so if you notice something that is not grammatically correct, you would be correct to assume that she tried to get me to change it, but I refused. I am a better writer because of her.
- Dex Greenbright is the wizard of all things visual, creating illustrations and the cover. When I saw the cover, I totally pumped both arms in the air and shouted "Yes!"
- A shout out of thanks to my alpha readers: Justin Hagen, Mark Mullozzi, and Cynthia Daigle. They gave me good feedback that helped this be a better book.
- As always, my marvelous wife, Joyce, who puts up with me spending hours at the computer and has always been my number one fan.
- Last, and most important, you, dear reader. There are lots of things to spend time on in today's world. I am grateful you spent a bit of that time with this book.

The I.T. Leader's First Days

AUTHOR BIO

John Bredesen has worked in IT for manufacturing companies for over 30 years. Working through system administrator, developer, and business analyst jobs, he spent most of those years leading IT professionals. His prior book, *The I.T. Leaders' Handbook*, covers the range of topics experienced IT leaders need to master. John lives in Minnesota, USA, where he enjoys his morning coffee, learning new technology, and setting his music volume to 11.

If you like this book, head on over to The-IT-Director.com and join the newsletter mailing list. John promises to keep the signal-to-noise ratio high and the Rush references low.

The I.T. Leader's First Days

NAMES FROM THE EXAMPLES

When recounting stories in a book, the author is faced with the decision on which names to use. If not the real names, what names do you use? I chose to use astronauts. Because I think space is cool. There is no relationship between the story told and the particular name used.

1. Ronald McNair, astronaut, died in the Space Shuttle Challenger disaster.
2. Stephanie D. Wilson, astronaut
3. Leland Melvin, astronaut
4. Mae C. Jemison, astronaut
5. Michael Anderson, astronaut

The I.T. Leader's First Days

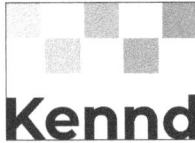

Kennd Publishing

Kennd Publishing is a US company based in Minnesota. Kennd publishes both fiction and non-fiction books that expand your horizons. For more information, visit Kennd-publishing.com or email info@kennd-publishing.com.

Related Books by Kennd Publishing

The I.T. Leaders' Handbook, John A. Bredesen, 2021

If you are an Information Technology (IT) manager, director, or CIO, this book will help you raise your game. Starting with foundations such as change management, technical debt, and categorizing the work, the book builds to cover important aspects of Business, People, and how to think about the ever-changing Technology IT needs to deal with.

The I.T. Leader's First Days, John A. Bredesen, 2022

Every leader starts out somewhere, and this book helps the new IT leader start strong. The book starts with basic skills that an IT leader needs and covers what the leader should do in their first few months on the job. The second half of the book is a distilled version of the Foundations, Business, People, and Technology sections from *The I.T. Leaders' Handbook*, rewritten for new IT Leaders.

The I.T. Leader's First Days

Index

The I.T. Leader's First Days

www.ingramcontent.com/pod-product-compliance
Lightning Source LLC
Chambersburg PA
CBHW071427210326
41597CB00020B/3692